T0287911

The Social Sciences and Theories of Race

The Social Sciences and Theories of Race

VERNON J. WILLIAMS JR.

University of Illinois Press
URBANA AND CHICAGO

Manufactured in the United States of America
1 2 3 4 5 C P 5 4 3 2 1
∞ This book is printed on acid-free paper.

Library of Congress Cataloging-in-Publication Data
Williams, Vernon J. The social sciences and theories of race /
Vernon J. Williams, Jr.
p. cm.
Includes bibliographical references and index.
ISBN-13: 978-0-252-03086-4 (cloth : alk. paper)
ISBN-10: 0-252-03086-9 (cloth : alk. paper)
ISBN-13: 978-0-252-07320-5 (pbk. : alk. paper)
ISBN-10: 0-252-07320-7 (pbk. : alk. paper)
1. Race relations—Philosophy.
2. Ethnicity—Philosophy.
3. African Americans—Social conditions.
I. Title.
HT1521.W54 2006
305.8'001—dc22 2005031547

For the Over-the-Hill Gang:
Jimmie L. Franklin
Rhett S. Jones
Charles Caston
Benjamin Daise
Wilson J. Moses

Contents

Acknowledgments

The seven essays contained within this volume were written over a period of a little more than two decades. Six of them have been previously published during the interim in books, anthologies, and journals—albeit in somewhat different forms. One of the essays is published in this collection for the first time. The focus of all seven pieces is on one or more aspects of anthropology's and sociology's rather sordid engagements with one of the ugliest of the United States' most enduring problems. Indeed, these derivative works are a result of further reflections on my previous research and writing during the past thirty years on race and race relations.

I would like to offer my sincere gratitude to the following scholars and autodidacts for providing me with constructive criticisms: Lee D. Baker, Richard Blanton, Diane Carlson, Charles Caston, Fay M. Chan, Benjamin Daise, Regna Darnell, Carolyn Fluehr-Lobban, V. P. Franklin, George M. Fredrickson, Faye V. Harrison, Rhett Jones, Harold Keltnick, Anthony J. Lemelle Jr., Genna Rae McNeill, Tatcho Mindiola, Wilson J. Moses, Robert Perrucci, Audrey Smedley, Karol Weaver, Phillip Wilford, Harold D. Woodman, and Drexel Woodson. My stubborn resistance to some of their pertinent criticisms makes me wholly responsible for whatever errors of facts and distortions of interpretations that are herein.

The Social Sciences and Theories of Race

Introduction

In his Bancroft Prize–winning book *A History of Negro Education in the South, from 1619 to the Present* (1968), sociologist and historian Henry A. Bullock, who taught both of my parents at Prairie View A and M College (now University) in the 1940s, and me more than two decades later at the University of Texas at Austin, wrote:

> Every book is somewhat autobiographical in nature. [The writer of this book is] like an artist who paints a picture or a composer who scores a symphony, and is moved to express an idea that haunts him [or her] and to share it with other people. A frank admission of this degree of personal bias is not dangerous, for reality is never absolute, but is always relative to the level from which it is observed. Though some element of the author's personality inescapably creeps into what he writes, his unique experiences within one of many private worlds may add another face to the multifaceted design that is human reality.[1]

At the time I read Professor Bullock's statements in 1968, they made good sense. Indeed, racial particularism matters—as it has throughout our nation's history—and it certainly affected my circuitous route to the study of race in the history of the behavioral sciences—specifically anthropology, sociology, and psychology. As a male of African American descent born and raised in the South, I was attracted to science, believing in the rhetoric of my idealistic science teachers at the Abraham Lincoln High School in La Marque, Texas: "If you become a good scientist, no one can prevent you from earning the highest distinction." Thus, as a teenager, I attended National Science Foundation summer programs in biology at two historically African American colleges: Wiley College in Marshall, Texas, in 1964, and

Grambling College (now University) in Grambling, Louisiana, in 1965. Although I enjoyed a degree of success at those endeavors, later, during my undergraduate years at the University of Texas at Austin between 1966 and 1969, I changed my course of study to literature, history, classical civilization, and philosophy. My interests in history and literature grew during my course work for the doctorate in American civilization at Brown University in the early 1970s. Had it not been for a misfortune that derailed all smidgens of respect for the traditional approaches to those disciplines in the humanities, I would perhaps still be pursuing a purblind path into esoteric antiquarianism.

Nevertheless, in my relentless quest for an innovative and groundbreaking dissertation topic, I was compelled by an assistant professor of anthropology (whose name I cannot recall) to read the books of historians of the American social sciences. In 1974, the same anthropologist introduced me to *Race, Culture, and Evolution* by George W. Stocking Jr. (1968). Fascinated by Stocking's precise usage of the English language and his technical virtuosity, I was also impressed with such lasting contributions as his discovery of neo-Lamarckian traits within turn-of-the-twentieth-century American racial thinking in the social sciences; his examination of the residue of polygenist thought in the writings of behavioral scientists in the aforesaid period; and his examination and analysis of the critique of racial formalism. Such statements as the following depict the strengths of his contributions:

> By the middle of the twentieth century, it was commonplace for educated Americans to refer to human differences in cultural terms, and to say that "modern science has shown that all human races are equal." In fact, what science has shown was better put negatively than positively; there was no scientific basis for assuming that one race was inferior or superior to another. . . . The data of human differences . . . was not supported by the evidence.[2]

Reputable scholars of the history of race during the 1960s—such as Thomas F. Gossett and I. A. Newby—concurred with Stocking's argument that stated that the paradigm of *absolute* white racial superiority was undermined by the demolition of evidence on which that bogus claim was made. For example, in *Race: The History of an Idea in America* (1963), Gossett stated: "Racism had developed into such a contradictory mass of the unprovable and the emotional that the serious students eventually recognized that as a source of explanation for mental and temperamental traits of a people it was worthless. Once this point was accepted, the top-heavy intellectual structures of racism began to topple, one after another."[3] The historian I. A. Newby has argued, in *Jim Crow's Defense: Anti-Negro Thought in Amer-*

ica, 1900–1930 (1965), that during the interwar years "reputable scientists and scholars . . . came to see environment as the source of racial inequality."[4] Thus, it has come as a rude awakening that John P. Jackson Jr., in his book *Social Scientists for Social Justice: Making the Case against Segregation* (2001), asserts that during the interwar years social scientists held that "all races had equal intellectual and physical abilities"; "what were previously viewed as *innate* racial differences . . . [were] only apparent *differences.*"[5]

Jackson's hyperbolic statements, it is essential to note, failed to deal with the skepticism—rather than advocacy of racial equality—that characterized behavioral scientific thought on the capabilities of African Americans. Scholars of race in the 1960s demonstrated that the paradigm of white racial superiority was undermined not by some assertion of African American equality, but rather by the demolition of the evidence on which the claim of the total innate inferiority of blacks was made. What historians of race and historically minded social scientists argue, in other words, is that their colleagues during the interwar years did not believe that the races were equal, but rather that there was no scientific basis for the claim of "absolute" white intellectual superiority. To put the argument more precisely, all whites were not assigned superior positions to all African Americans, yet anthropologists and sociologists held that the average intelligence of most African Americans was lower than that of most European Americans and that African Americans would not produce proportionally as many—to use the words of the premier anthropologist of his day, Franz Boas—"men of high genius" as European Americans would. In short, anthropologists and sociologists spoke in terms of "approximate equality," "virtual equality," and "individual differences" rather than in the language of African American racial equality. In essence, behavioral scientists during the interwar years still clung—as the anthropologist John L. Jackson Jr. stated lucidly in *Harlem World: Doing Race and Class in Contemporary Black American* (2001)—to "anthropometrics to argue for aggregate differences between races. . . . [T]his same argument has been updated without Boas's liberal leanings in Charles Murray and Richard Herrnstein's *The Bell Curve.*"[6]

By adhering to a reified notion of biological race as real and as a consequence subject to historical and scientific investigation, behavioral scientists have indeed aided and abetted the promulgation of *moot* issues. For at issue during the past three centuries are ethical problems that often require a leap of faith that clouds the eyeballs of even the strictest methodological purist.

As a consequence, this book of essays examines and analyzes Franz Boas, George W. Ellis, Booker T. Washington, Ulysses G. Weatherly, and Monroe N. Work—men whose ideas on race and culture continally evolved during the Age of Jim Crow. Indeed, in this collection of essays I seek to demonstrate that these persons were not permanently enmeshed in static categories, but were sophisticated anthropologists, sociologists, and social thinkers who learned from what they read and from their contact with other able scholars on both sides of the color lines, and who reflected on the inexorable social forces to which they were exposed. In short, in this work these scholars are depicted as developing, changing, and making significant contributions to the idea that culture was a powerful force.

In attempting to exhume explanations of how and why their ideas on race and culture evolved as they did, I draw on the intellectual, personal, and social forces at work on my subjects. As a consequence, I ignore the boundaries separating cultural history, biography, autobiography, social history, and intellectual history in order to provide the reader with evidence to support my conclusions—with the hope that I have provided the fullest possible picture of these social scientists. These individuals, who had many of the same interests, values, and working assumptions—albeit in distinct ways—responded to the insights on race and culture that the newly emerging social sciences (anthropology, sociology, and psychology) provided.

Suffice it to say that these essays add incrementally to my developing theory of social change (chapters 1 and 4), which emphasizes the external social and political pressures and the ethnic origins of the social scientists themselves, as opposed to the internal methodological controls and intellectual rigor of the dominant practitioners of anthropology and sociology. Despite the rationalism of social scientists, their conflicts over values cannot be ignored by competent experts who have studied the history of their disciplines and attempted to uncover their fundamental *raison d'être*.

Part 1, which is divided into three essays, examines three distinct and discrete discourses surrounding not only anthropology's "skeletons in the closet" but also its resiliency and latent potentiality. Chapter 1 resurrects the oppositional yet fecund subaltern tradition of ethnology and ethnography of black Westerners during the nineteenth and twentieth centuries. It seeks to polemicize the necessity of constructing more inclusive narratives of anthropology's history. Although it is the case that an overemphasis on the agency of black Westerners obscures the extent to which most white practitioners of "racial science" were able to silence, through their sophistry, black thinkers during the nineteenth and early twentieth centuries, the emphasis in this essay on black Westerners' traditions recovers the alternative subtraditions that perhaps could have spared generations of budding scholars (both nonwhite and white, both male and female) an unnecessary and damaging sense of rootlessness that continues to bedevil many of them.

Chapter 2 analyzes and examines Regna Darnell's statement that "the physical anthropology of Franz Boas has had its continuous impact on the central place of race and racism in Boas's theory of culture,"[7] and is a continuation of my earlier work on the father of American professional anthropology.

Chapter 3 analyzes and examines the subaltern tradition of African American anthropology as manifested in George Washington Ellis's study of West African peoples at the turn of the twentieth century. It clearly demonstrates the intersection of hegemonic with subaltern traditions in American anthropology and underscores a significant figure whose important contributions have been subject to erasure.

The inclusion of nonwhite men and women and white women—or diversification, if you will—in the historiography of anthropology will help to expand the canon of American intellectual history and pave the way for more inclusive narratives. Suffice it to say that the spate of excellent books and articles published on the anthropology of race and race relations since the early 1990s indicates that at this juncture, the process of expanding the discourse is well under way.

Part 2, which is divided into four essays, centers on what Louis Wirth called his "love": "the field of race relations." Chapter 4 is an attempt to challenge traditional internalist orthodoxies that attribute the decline of "racist" thinking in the discipline of sociology solely to internalist developments. Although my argument tends to reify the volitional potency of great minds, in the social sciences it clearly demonstrates that the aforesaid eradication of racism also was a byproduct of political factors, ethnic identities, and supraindividual social structural forces affecting the lives of "great minds" in the urban-industrial areas in which they lived and worked.

Chapter 5 is intended to depict Booker T. Washington's transitions from a benign racial essentialism to an espousal of Anglo-American cultural essentialism and finally to Afrocentrism. In doing so, it is my intention to extirpate the core of Washington's imbricated approaches that are reflected in pre–World War II sociology.

Chapter 6 centers on Hoosier sociologist Ulysses G. Weatherly, who argued that African culture was eradicated by slavery in America and that as a consequence African Americans were a pliable people, readily influenced by whatever social forces to which they were subjected. He drew on Washington's emphasis on European and European American cultural essentialism in order to rationalize some of the most repressive practices of Anglo-Americans in the name of cultural homogeneity, both at home and abroad, and to influence United States foreign policy.

Chapter 7 seeks to demonstrate how Washington's cultural essentialism resurfaces in Monroe Nathan Work's libertarian-conservative uplift ideology, which contradicted some of his early liberal propensities.

In short, those southern, African American, and European American persons who are the subjects of the majority of these essays contributed significantly to the early sociology of race relations and have paved the way for expanding the discourse in sociology in reference to race and ethnic relations. Thus, these persons have made possible the fruition of more inclusive narratives of their discipline.

PART I

Race, Culture, and Anthropology

1 Historiographical Concerns in the History of Anthropology

Since the late 1960s, George W. Stocking Jr., professor emeritus of anthropology at the University of Chicago, has—with only occasional lapses—pursued a strictly internalist methodological approach to the historical investigation of the European and European American behavioral sciences.[1] Stocking's books, edited volumes, and articles have withstood both the initial criticisms and the tests of time. Indeed, the longevity and durability of his contributions are testaments to the acuity of his keen mind.[2]

Typical of Stocking's influence on the methodological orientation of scholars of the history of science is Nancy L. Stepan's defense of his internalist position in her book *The Idea of Race in Science: Great Britain, 1800–1960* (1982). At that time, Stepan made the case—in an even stronger and more precise fashion than Stocking himself—when she wrote: "Social and political factors . . . did not determine directly the specific form scientific arguments took about race." Furthermore, scientific arguments, Stepan added, "were instead derived from procedures and the content of the sciences themselves."[3] Unwittingly, however—as the great historian of race George M. Fredrickson pointed out to me in 1983, while I was an unpaid associate in the history department at Northwestern University—Stepan's book suggests that British scientists and social scientists were unable or unwilling to pursue a more enlightened path on the issue of race at the turn of the twentieth century, primarily because social structural changes in Great Britain were not sufficiently wrenching to compel them to reassess their positions on the issues of race and race relations.

Furthermore, since the mid-1970s, I have raised serious doubts about the full adequacy of the explanatory potency of the strictly internalist discourse in reference to the issue of race in the behavioral sciences. As a consequence, in my book *From a Caste to a Minority* (1989), I sought to make the case for the saliency of external social structural forces in compelling sociologists to adopt anthropologist Franz Boas's liberal environmentalist stance on the issues of the character and capabilities of African Americans.[4] Nonetheless, the question of why the Boasian revolution took place so early in anthropology was not addressed. As a consequence, I tackled this issue in *Rethinking Race* (1996) and concluded that although the internal discourse in anthropology was certainly important, it was not sufficient in and of itself to compel reassessment of older theories of race and race relations. In other words, cataclysmic social structural changes were necessary preconditions for the initial triumph of antiracist thinking in the newly emerging American behavioral sciences (anthropology, sociology, and psychology).

Nevertheless, many historically minded students of the behavioral sciences have an aversion to externalist argumentation. Instead, they themselves write polemics on the raucousness of the identity politics in their disciplines. These scholars think they have sound reasons to be nostalgic and to lament, primarily because the "good old days" of the cold-blooded, "objective" search for "truth" have supposedly been distanced and drowned out by the clamor of a particularistic-oriented group of new scholars who—to use the words of anthropologist Hubert S. Lewis—believe that "they have a new and better way to understand reality than their teachers and predecessors," who seem to them to have been "hopelessly old-fashioned, wrong-headed, and on the wrong track." Although I concur in Lewis's argument for the abiding need for fair examinations in the history of the behavioral sciences, the same standards that are applied to subaltern traditions, I argue, should be applied to the mongers of "objectivity" and their acolytes.

Even more disturbing, however, are Lewis's hyperbolic statements that attribute present-day ideological clashes to a generational divide. Such arguments ignore the transformation in the history of anthropology since Stocking's statements in 1992 in which he admitted that most of his career had been devoted to the narration of "figures in hegemonic anthropological traditions."[5] Stocking's humility before the inexorable ebb and flux of time is manifest when he admits that the necessity of studying "other alternative histories" and of rescuing "neglected precursors of paradigmatic alternatives once lost and now to be regained" is a noble endeavor.[6]

Stocking's observations were made at about the same time that several scholars of anthropology were attempting to uncover subaltern and oppositional traditions in order to justify—to use anthropologist Faye V. Harrison's words—"projects committed to decolonizing and democratizing anthropology . . . [that also] acknowledge and come to terms with anthropology's gender and social politics." Nevertheless, there are schisms even among the ideological factions that advocate the necessity of producing, in Harrison's words, "synthesis incorporating elements from political economy, reflexive and interpretive ethnography, a race and class-conscious feminism, and radical traditions of scholarship by blacks and other peoples of color both inside and outside the West."[7] The anthropologist Micaela di Leonardo, like Harrison, argues that expanding the canon is a laudable undertaking yet is pessimistic about the contemporary significance of such efforts. The "demand of the triumph of *fin de siécle* imperialist racism," di Leonardo argues cogently, "or of the recent solidification of the Right and its national and international entailments, prevents emancipatory analysis altogether."[8]

Far more productive for scholarly engagement than either Stocking's or Harrison's optimism or di Leonardo's pessimism is an obscure article published in 1980 in *Black Scholar:* "Anthropology and the Black Experience," by the late distinguished anthropologist St. Clair Drake (1911–1990). This historical adumbration of work by black Western practitioners of ethnology and ethnography during the nineteenth century and of the discipline of anthropology in the twentieth century foreshadowed some of the most pressing concerns in the history of anthropology's confrontation with the issues of race. Indeed, although this article's full significance has rarely been acknowledged, subsequent writings about the history of anthropology build on Drake's perspective, evidence, and argument.

Drake's observation that nineteenth-century "Egyptology was on the cutting edge of the fight against racism" deserves attention, if for no other reason than its spawning of what historian Wilson J. Moses labels "Egyptocentrism"; that is, the "process" of assigning traditional American racial constructs to the peoples of ancient Egypt.[9] Along with Moses, several historians, including Stephen Howe, Mia Bay, Maghan Keita, and Clarence Walker, have recently documented the fascination (both past and present) of African Americans with Egyptology as an antidote to the racism of European and European American scholars.[10]

Moses argued in 1995 about Afrocentrism that, "like most mythologies, it is only half an attempt on the part of respectable, honest people to create a positive folk mythology."[11] British author Stephen Howe asserted in 1998 that certain types of Egyptocentrism are a "kind of 'anti-universalism'" that is a "valuable—indeed, essential corrective to European cultural pretensions and distortions of history."[12] Mia Bay in 2000 observed that "Afrocentrism's glorification of the African and Egyptian origins of the black race has its own origin in the racial thought of nineteenth-century black intellectuals, who in many cases took pen to paper for the primary purpose of defending the common ancestry of the human family against white racists who sought to argue that blacks descended from a separate creation."[13] In 2001, Keita demonstrated how "variegated," "complex," and rich in theoretical and historical concepts were the motley crew of writers in the nineteenth centuries.[14] Even Clarence E. Walker, who argues that in the present, "Afrocentrism constitutes a form of totalitarian group thinking," nevertheless admits that "Afrocentrism may at one time have been innocent and devoid of political ramifications."[15]

It should be noted, however, that at that historical juncture, Drake gave short shrift to Egyptology. He paid far more attention to the ethnological and ethnographic writings of black Westerners, such as Martin R. Delany, Edward Wilmot Blyden, George Washington Ellis, and William Shepard-Persons, whose works, in Drake's words, countered "the flood of derogatory propaganda that began to spew forth" in nineteenth-century North America and Europe.[16]

In recent years, scholars such as Wilson, Moses, Carolyn Fluehr-Lobban, Bay, and Keita have documented the valiant effort on the part of black Westerners, varying as widely as Haitian ethnologist Anténor Firmin and United States–born Episcopalian missionary Alexander Crummel, to subvert the propaganda of European and European American scholars. These black Westerners embraced an intellectual blend of what the historically minded anthropologist Lee D. Baker labels conflicting variants of egalitarianism, romantic racialism, and monoculturalism.

Historians of the subaltern tradition of black Westerners' anthropology that Drake sketched out have uncovered an oppositional yet fecund tradition of resistance on the part of black Westerners to the dominant "scientific" discourse on race during the nineteenth and early twentieth centuries. Thus, although most white practitioners of racial science were able to silence the opposition of black thinkers, historians such as Bay, Sander L. Gilman and Nancy Leys Stepan; Moses and historically minded anthropologists such as Lee D. Baker, Ira E. Harrison, and Faye V. Harrison; and Fluehr-Lobban are filling out the narratives of anthropology's history.[17]

In some of my previously published works I have focused on George Washington Ellis. These short pieces centered almost exclusively on his scholarly classic *Negro Culture in West Africa,* published in 1914.[18] In those writings I observed that Ellis's book received a warm reception in its day, especially from some of the leading African American and European American authorities on the issues of race and race relations. Kelly Miller, a prominent member of the African American intelligentsia and dean of the College of Arts and Sciences at Howard University, who had in 1912 introduced sociology to his students at his institution, declared that Ellis's study of the Vai people of Liberia was based on "a careful personal study of the habits, manners, social customs and usage of the people whom he undertakes to describe."[19] Miller went on to observe that the book was "profoundly interesting to students of the African situation" and concluded that "unlike armchair cultural evolutionists one feels the author is speaking with the weight of personal authority."[20] The venerable W. E. B. Du Bois, who had communicated and given encouragement to Ellis when he was gathering his data, was far more emphatic than Miller, asserting: "This history ought to be in every American library."[21] Furthermore, two newspapers in the northeastern United States declared their approval of the high quality of Ellis's scholarly work. "Mr. Ellis," the Boston *Transcript* wrote, "has given excellent and valuable contribution to the history of the Negro Race."[22] Finally, the New York *Sun* commented that the book was " a very valuable contribution to the history of the Negro Race."[23] It should be noted that Ellis (as well as his publisher) had hoped to reach a larger and broader readership; yet much to his dismay, that book, like many scholarly works, was a commercial failure. To his credit, he also disseminated his findings on the character and capabilities of West Africans in other media. What is remarkable is his persistent efforts to educate both African Americans and European Americans on a subject regarding which the academy as well as the general public were mired in ignorance.

As early as 1911, Ellis published the long, two-part article "African News and Stories: Interest, Folklore and African Stories" in the *Fellowship Herald: Organ of the Negro Fellowship League.* Furthermore, from his return to the United States in 1910 to his death in 1919, Ellis was a contributing editor to the *Journal of Race Development,* a quasi-scholarly periodical edited by Alexander Chamberlain, the first person to receive a doctorate under Franz Boas. In addition, he wrote a second-rate vanity novel, *The Leopard's Spots* (1917), that purportedly treated "love and adventure in the West African jungle." Furthermore, his attempts to enlighten scholars and the broader public on West Africa were not confined solely to the written media. During his stay in Liberia, Ellis acquired a large collection of African art that he loaned to the Smithsonian Institute in Washington, D.C. These artifacts ultimately were donated to Fisk University by Ellis's sister in 1951.

Fortunately, during the twentieth century's first two decades, Franz Boas engendered a shift in scholarly discourse concerning the character and capabilities of blacks in both Africa and the West. Boas became an effective advocate for scientific antiracism during the twenty years *after* his affiliation with Columbia University circa 1896. Boas's scientific research involved attempts to recruit and train as anthropologists racially diverse cohorts.

It is thus a tribute to Ira Harrison, Faye V. Harrison, and their collaborators in *African American Pioneers in Anthropology* that they have, in Faye Harrison's words, offered "response to the expanded space and critical possibilities created by the disruption and transfigurations in the discipline since the 1960s." The Harrisons and their collaborators have focused on the lives, thoughts, and actions of leading African American practitioners of anthropology—both men and women—in the twentieth century. They have celebrated the triumphs of individuals who succeeded in accomplishing much, despite the odds and the obdurateness of classism, sexism, and racism. These scholars do not underestimate the extent to which individuals, such as Caroline Bond Day, Zora Neale Hurston, Louis Eugene King, Laurence Foster, and W. Montague Cobb, have succeeded in making outstanding contributions to anthropology and beyond. They do not underestimate, however, the extent to which, as late as the 1970s, individuals' options, such as those of St. Clair Drake, Allison Davis, William S. Willis Jr., and Hubert B. Ross, were limited and circumscribed by European Americans—an obvious consequence of the caste-like structure in American higher education. In essence, Ira Harrison and Faye V. Harrison's anthology has presented this reader with much important new information, not only in reference to the agency of African Americans (for they have narrated their achievements and contribution to the evisceration of Eurocentrism) but also their victimization in a discipline torn between universalism and particularism.

Furthermore, in reference to anthropology itself and the issue of race, Lee D. Baker's book *From Savage to Negro* (1998) and Thomas C. Paterson's book *A Social History of Anthropology in the United States* (2001) have given significant attention to extracognitive, ideological, sociopolitical, and ethical dimensions of the major agents in their discipline. They concur in the argument that anthropological knowledge, according to Paterson, "is shaped by what the world is and who the anthropologists and the diverse peoples they study are."[24] Suffice it to say that when all of the layers of jargon, statistics, and deconstruction endemic to the discipline of anthropology are unmasked, the worldviews of scholars reveal a dialectic between the internal concerns peculiar to scholars in the discipline and the external trends, events, and people that evoke stress among educated persons in our nation, thus needlessly complicating our world.

Indeed, on the issue of black Westerners' presence in the discipline (for it certainly has skeletons in the closet in reference to this issue), anthropology has not exhibited the degree of continuity that one might presume if one focused solely on Boas's pioneering yet futile efforts to diversify the racial composition of his students. Nevertheless, some of anthropology's leading practitioners (both black and white) are making a concerted push to reinvigorate Boas's early mission. We must pay an enormous tribute to Ira Harrison and Faye V. Harrison and their compatriots who are fleshing out Drake's outline of black Westerners' contributions to race in an anthology, for by pursuing scholarship that compels anthropologists to rethink their precursors' narratives and broaden their concerns, a more inclusive vision of their work *might* be attained.

2 Franz Boas's Paradox and the African American Intelligentsia

During the past five decades, several scholars have celebrated the monumental role that Franz "Uri" Boas played in initiating a social scientific revolution on the issue of race. In earlier publications, I sought to demonstrate that he slowly emerged as an enlightened apostle of antiracism—only after he virtually had nullified the significance of anthropometric measurements of cranial capacities in his assessments of the capabilities of blacks and had experienced prolonged contacts with members of the African American intelligentsia.

This essay, which explores Boas's changing thought on African Americans, is marked on one end by Boas's first extended conceptualization of the "Negro Problem" in an address entitled "Human Faculty as Determined by Race," published in 1894, and on the other end by his final extended discussion of African Americans in the last edition of *The Mind of Primitive Man,* published in 1938. It seeks to substantiate three arguments. First, I concur in the argument that Boas's assessment of his anthropometric measurements changed progressively over time. Nevertheless, as late as 1915, Boas's racial vision was restricted by severe limitations. His attempts to make inferences concerning the capabilities of African Americans led him to conclude that there might be slight differences in the direction of the hereditary aptitudes of blacks and whites—for example, in music. Second, I will demonstrate that Boas's analysis of prejudice and his particularistic, rational scientific approach to Africans led him to conclude that discrimination was the salient variable in American race relations. Indeed, Boas was forward-looking when he attacked the problems of prejudice and argued that individual merit, not race, should determine what class position individual blacks should attain in American society. Third, I will argue that despite the schisms in Boas's writing on race up until 1938, his position changed and evolved; his positions on race were dynamic. He was always conscious of the growing impact that African Americans were having upon the nation's economic, social, and cultural life and conscious also of the increase in anti-Semitism in this environment. Thus, one of the most obvious results of my research demonstrates the conflict between science and ideology in the thought of Boas. An adherent to a naturalistic worldview, as new empirically verifiable data were uncovered by other scholars, Boas's points of view in reference to the condition and destiny of African Americans changed and evolved on some issues, but remained intact on others. This is not to say the issues were strictly scientific and not political, but to suggest that Boas's political awakening was as mutually reinforcing as his empirical research. Put another way, "political beliefs" were as salient as "scientific commitments" in countering the claims of overt racists.

After 1915 Boas not only used the liberal environmentalist argument to dispel the myth of "racial hereditary characteristics" but also acted as adviser to Melville Herskovits, Otto Klineberg, Ruth Benedict, Zora Neale Hurston, Margaret Mead, and Ashley Montagu—persons who built on and disseminated the Boasian perspectives on the capabilities of African Americans, prejudice, and the achievements of Africans, not only in physical anthropology, cultural anthropology, and literature but also in the broad public arena from the 1910s to the 1960s. Furthermore, Boas transformed the thought of members of the African American intelligentsia, such as Booker T. Washington, W. E. B. Du Bois, Monroe N. Work, George W. Ellis, Carter G. Woodson, George E. Haynes, Alain LeRoy Locke, Charles S. Johnson, Charles H. Thompson, Abram Harris, and Zora Neale Hurston. Indeed, "it was in the area of race," as Marshall Hyatt has concluded, "that Boas had his greatest impact on American and on future intellectual thought."[1]

Put simply, Boas—albeit grudgingly—attempted to extricate race relations theory from *most* of the racist assumptions of late nineteenth-century social science. Once Boas had established that white prejudice, not the assumed innate racial traits, was the major obstacle to black progress, after 1930 it became exceedingly difficult in anthropology and sociology to rationalize the caste-like system in the United States on the assumed congenital inferiority of people of West and Central African descent. In sum, flowing from what I call the "Boasian paradox"—the contradiction between philosophically egalitarian sentiments and his recontextualization of traditional European physical anthropology—was a prescriptive statement; that is, in a just society African Americans should *approximate,* not assume, a distribution proportional to their size in the population in each socioeconomic class in the United States. Thus, despite his imprisonment in the racist paradigm of late nineteenth-century physical anthropology, which stated that blacks were physically different from and somewhat inferior to whites, Boas at times succeeded in qualifying the inferences drawn from the empirical data to suggest that racism had shaky foundations; he thereby first adumbrated the position of modern-day liberals on the issue of the destiny of African Americans in the social order of the United States. Indeed, Boas felt that once they resolved their problem of group identity, African Americans *could* be assimilated.

* * *

The father of modern American anthropology was born into a liberal Jewish household in Minden, Westphalia, Germany, on July 9, 1858, a decade following the republican revolutions that swept Europe. It was clear by Boas's birth date that the revolutions, characterized by an emphasis on liberalism and the creation of democratic republican nations, had failed. Nevertheless, Boas's parents—his father, Meier, a successful merchant, and his mother, Sophie, the founder of the first Froebel Kindergarten in Minden—were the close associates of many prominent "forty-eighters," such as Carl Schurz and Abraham Jocobi, who married Sophie's younger sister. In such a setting, Boas was inculcated with the liberal ideals of the revolution of 1848—ideals to which he held firmly throughout his life. So intense was the fervor for the ideals of the revolution of 1848 in the Boas household that their Jewish background had few direct intellectual consequences for the young Franz. Although Boas, as Marshall Hyatt has pointed out, "was raised an orthodox Jew," Boas later recalled that his religious education "was purely a sop for his grandparents, who were orthodox." According to Boas, his "parents had broken through the shackles of dogma." "My father," he continued, "had retained an emotional affection for the ceremonial in his parental home, without allowing it to influence his intellectual freedom. Thus I was spared the struggle against religious dogma that besets the lives of so many young people." Nevertheless, Boas's ethnicity was important and had a decisive impact on his later anthropology and politics.[2]

As was customary in Germany during this period, Boas attended several universities: Heidelberg, Bonn, and Kiel. He was awarded the doctorate in physics with a minor in geography at Kiel in 1881. His dissertation, *Contributions to the Understanding of the Color of Water,* sought to determine the intensities of light that struck different types of water. Confronting the problem of subjectivism when he tried to distinguish between two lights that produced slight differences in the color of two different types of water, Boas recalled in 1939 that the experiments suggested to him that "there are domains of our experience in which the concepts of quantity . . . with which I was accustomed to operate are not applicable."[3] Questions concerning the relativity of experience and the relationship between the physiological and the physical were two major philosophical problems he would confront in his later anthropological work.

After an uneventful year at Berlin University and another year in the German army, Boas studied and waited in vain for a teaching position in the increasingly conservative and anti-Semitic academic community in Bismarck's Germany. Disappointed, he went to Baffinland in 1883 to write a book. Although the transition from physics to ethnology, as George W. Stocking Jr. has demonstrated, "was not abrupt," his experience among the Eskimos sowed the seeds for his attempt to understand the laws of human nature some two years later. His field experience among the Eskimos was important, compelling him to change disciplines. After his return, while working at the Ethnological Museum, Boas wrote:

> After a long intercourse with the Eskimo, it was with feelings of sorrow and regret that I parted from my Arctic friends. I had seen that they enjoy life, and a hard life, as we do; that nature is also beautiful to them; that feelings of friendship also root in the Eskimo heart; that, although the character of their life is so rude as compared to civilized life, the Eskimo is a man as we are; that his feelings, his virtues and his shortcomings are based in human nature, like ours.[4]

Boas's ambivalence—the tension between his "philosophical egalitarianism" and his cultural chauvinism that is obvious in the above passage—toward the Eskimos would later be reflected in his statements on African Americans.

Seeking better career opportunities in which to pursue ethnology, Boas emigrated to the United States in 1887, yet he suffered tremendous setbacks in his attempts to secure employment in Anglo-American-dominated institutions. Virulent anti-Semitism pervaded the nation when Boas entered the country. Jews of German descent, who had begun to be affected by anti-Semitism as early as the 1880s, witnessed a decline of their status. Later, during the 1890s, their opportunities in Anglo-American-dominated institutions and housing were narrowed, a direct product of the influx of large numbers of eastern European Jews after the 1880s. His post as geographical editor of *Science* was not funded in 1888; he was forced to resign a position as a docent in physical anthropology at Clark University in 1892; and he was dismissed from a temporary position as chief assistant of anthropology at the World's Fair Columbia Exposition in Chicago in 1894. William Rainey Harper, president of the University of Chicago, refused to offer him a professorship in 1894, citing Boas's inability to "take direction" as one of the reasons behind his decision. In 1894, Boas was unemployed and mourning the death of his young daughter.

In sum, when Boas delivered his outgoing address as vice-president of Section H of the American Association for the Advancement of Science in Brooklyn, New York, in August 1894, he was expressing liberal convictions that flowed from a worldview that was unique in the United States—convictions that were a direct product of the remnants of liberal ideals in Germany, his scientific training, and his marginal status in the anthropological community. Furthermore, this attack on the racist orthodoxy permeating both European and American social scientific communities was bound inextricably to the so-called Negro problem in both the North and South and the virulent anti-Semitism that pervaded the nation.

In the context of the turn-of-the-century United States, extreme and irrational Negrophobia pervaded every aspect of the nation's life and was a formidable obstacle to a rational discussion of the condition of African Americans. The reconciliation between the North and South that had taken place in 1877 had resulted in the subordination of blacks in the South by the early 1880s. As a consequence, the period from roughly 1890 until 1920, despite the economic gains that some blacks made, was one of the lowest points in the history of white-black relations in the United States. Indeed, through disfranchisement, Jim Crow laws, extralegal violence, and the removal of blacks from skilled labor, whites had consolidated their higher caste-like position by 1900. In the North, these forms of blatant racism had been less extreme, yet prejudice and discrimination had exacerbated the social problems of blacks and stymied their progress. Suffice it to say that developments in the area of "race relations" of the period were some of the most shameful episodes in recent American history. The level of the discussion of the intellectual capabilities of African Americans was an obstacle that Boas, because of his adherence to physical anthropological background assumptions, had the most difficulty surmounting. The most significant myths espoused in the dominant discourse stated that African Americans were a homogeneous race whose low status in American society was due to their defective ancestry and/or an instinctive white prejudice, which prevented them from contributing to society, or "the mores," which excluded them from communal life with Euro-Americans.[5]

In "Human Faculty as Determined by Race," Boas presented views that George W. Stocking Jr. and Marshall Hyatt claimed were the genesis of themes that Boas pursued throughout the rest of his career. Although I concur in Hyatt's argument that Boas's ethnic status was the primary motivating force behind his attacks on anti-Negro prejudice, it should be noted that "Human Faculty as Determined by Race" contains sections infused with Boas's own bigotry toward African Americans as well. Rationalizing Boas's bigotry in 1968, Stocking has written: "Given the atmospheric pervasiveness of the idea of European racial superiority, it is hardly surprising that Boas wrote as a skeptic of received belief rather than a staunch advocate of racial equipotentiality. Despite his basic liberal humanitarian outlook, he was a white-skinned European writing for other white-skinned Europeans at the turn of century, and he was a physical anthropologist to boot."

In 1974, Stocking pointed out that "one is struck by the limits of Boas' critique in 1894." Although Stocking is aware of Boas's limitations, he has suggested that those limitations in no way detract from the fundamental Boasian stance in reference to race.[6] It is curious that Boas's analysis of the physical characteristics of blacks and his "men of high genius" hypothesis, which can be found in a Boas publication as late as 1938, contains several biases that detract from his stature as a philosophical egalitarian.

Boas's assessments of racial determinist arguments in the various branches of the social sciences were divided in 1894. On the one hand, he demonstrated the primacy of cultural determinants in accounting for historical achievements and the psychological makeup of different races. On the other hand, he conceded to racists by insisting that physical anthropological assumptions of the direct relation between intelligence and brain weight or cranial capacity were relevant. Boas even thought bodily form might have certain influences on the psychological makeup of races. The schism between the values of cultural determinism and racial determinism was the major weakness in his philosophical position on race. The schism was a direct product of his methodological rigor. Although Boas's sentiments resonated with his penchant for emphasizing cultural determinism, he still could not reconcile those sentiments with physical anthropological assumptions about racial differences. The tension is evident in his analysis of racial determinism from historical and physical anthropological perspectives.

From a historical perspective, the young Boas attacked the paradigm of the proponents of the comparative method. By assuming that there was a direct relationship between a race's achievements and the intellectual capacities of its members, the evolutionary anthropologists had essentially confounded achievement with an aptitude for achievement. Similarly, they judged any deviation from the white type as "a characteristic feature of a lower type." Boas insisted that the superiority of Western civilization could be accounted for on grounds other than those that suggest the superiority of the white race's mental faculty. He argued that other races, such as the Indians of Peru and Central America, had evolved into civilizations that were similar to that from which European civilization had its origins. However, European civilization, favored by the "common physical appearance, contiguity of habitat and modern differences in modes of manufacture" of its inhabitants, spread rapidly. When European civilization came into contact with races outside its domain, assimilation of nonwhites was difficult because of "striking differences of racial types, the preceding and the greater advance in civilization." The advocates of northern and western European superiority, he stressed, had ignored the fact that their civilization, which arose under favorable circumstances and spread rapidly, had "cut short" the development of non-European civilization "without regard to the people whom it was developing." The evolutionists' historical explanation of the low status of nonwhites was wrong, because "historical events rather than race appear to have been much more potent in leading races to civilization than their faculty, and it follows the achievements of races do not warrant us to assume that one race is more highly gifted than the others."[7]

Boas's criticisms of the evolutionists had exposed the ethnocentric fallacy of ranking nonwhite societies according to the characteristics they shared with European and American civilizations and revealed his cosmopolitan and liberal sentiments. But his evaluation of racial intellectual differences from the physical anthropological framework was infused with concessions to staunch racists. In the 1880s and early 1890s, Boas had been influenced significantly by the works of prominent Continental physical anthropologists, such as Paul Broca and Paul Topinard, and directly by Rudolph Virchow, with whom he had contact at the meetings of the Berlin Anthropological Society in 1882. Furthermore, throughout his career Boas was certain that physical anthropological data could clarify important ethnological questions.[8] Boas worked within the essentialist framework developed by Broca, the father of modern physical anthropology, who wrote in 1873 in reference to a table he had illustrated: "The table shows that West Africans have a cranial capacity about 100 c.c. less than the European races. To this figure we may add the following: Caffirs, Nubians, Tasmanians, Hottentots, Australians. These examples are sufficient to prove that if the volume of the cranium does not play a decisive role in the ranking of the races, it nevertheless has a very real importance."[9]

Thus, Boas speculated on the early jargon of the discipline that "it would seem that the greater the central nervous system, the higher the faculty of the race and the greater its aptitude to mental achievement." According to Boas, there were two methods useful in determining the size of the central nervous system: one could measure either the weight of the brain (which provided the most "accurate results") or the size of the cranial cavity. He conceded that both the brain weight and cranial cavities of whites, on average, were "larger than that of most other races, particularly larger than that of the Negroes."[10] Boas's conclusions were not new. As early as the 1840s, the "American School" of anthropology, of which Samuel George Morton, Josiah C. Nott, and George R. Gliddon were among the members, had based a major part of its proslavery defense on the comparative measurements of the cranial cavities of blacks and whites.[11]

Despite Boas's physical anthropological assumptions, he exercised considerable restraint in interpreting the data that were based solely on the relatively simple mathematical techniques of means, medians, and percentiles. On a visit to England in 1889, he had become acquainted with Sir Francis Galton. He appropriated the eugenicist's science of biometrics and used it to demonstrate that the "frequency distribution" of the cranial cavities of blacks and whites overlapped. He pointed out that Topinard's measurements revealed that 55 percent of Europeans, compared to 58 percent of "African Negroes," had cavities in the range of 1,450 to 1,650 cubic centimeters; however, the range greater than 1,550 cubic centimeters enclosed 50 percent of the whites and 27 percent of the blacks. His inference: "We might, therefore, anticipate a lack of men of high genius [among the Negroes] but should not anticipate any lack of faculty among the great mass of Negroes living among whites and enjoying the leadership of the best men of the race."[12]

The statement reflects obvious tension between liberal humanitarian sentiments and the ideas of racism. On the one hand, he implied strongly that blacks would produce proportionately fewer men capable of shaping either the nation's or the world's higher affairs; on the other hand, he was arguing for the significance of individual differences regardless of a person's race. *All* blacks, in other words, were not intellectually inferior to *all* whites, yet disproportionately few had the mental faculty requisite to shape the course of history.

Indeed, in 1894 the distinction between the position of Boas and that of ethnocentricists in institutions dominated by persons of British ancestry was slight. Illustrative of this argument are statements regarding the ape-like physical characteristics of the "Negro" by the leading "scientific" authorities on race at the turn of the century. Nathaniel S. Shaler, Kentucky-born professor of paleontology at Harvard, in 1890 stated unequivocally that the Negro was "nearer to the anthropoid or pre-human ancestry of man." In 1896 Edward D. Cope, a Pennsylvania-born Quaker and professor of geology and mineralogy at the University of Pennsylvania, argued that the Negro was ape-like because of his flat nose, his jaws that projected beyond the upper part of the face, his facial angle, "the deficiency of the calf of the leg, and the obliquity of the pelvis." Daniel G. Brinton, a former medical doctor who was appointed professor of linguistics and folklore at the University of Pennsylvania, was typical of northern white supremacists in anthropology who thought the Negro had ape-like characteristics. "The adult who retains the more numerous fetal, infantile or simian traits," he wrote in 1890, "is unquestionably inferior to him whose development has progressed beyond them. . . . Measured by these criteria the European or white race stands at head of the list, the African or Negro at its foot."[13] In sum, most European and American physical anthropologists believed that the Negro was an ape-like barbarian in their midst whose physique prevented him from attaining civilization.

When speaking of physical characteristics of blacks in "Human Faculty as Determined by Race," Boas clearly manifested the arrogance of his contemporaries when he wrote:

> We found that the face of the Negro as compared to the skull is larger than that of the American, whose face is in turn larger than that of the white. The lower portion of the face assumes larger dimensions. The alveolar arch is pushed forward and thus gains an appearance which reminds us of the higher apes. There is no denying that this feature is a most constant character of the black races representing a type slightly nearer the animal than the European type.

Nevertheless, using the tools of science on the basis of all the anthropometric measurements he could obtain on the various races, Boas concluded: "We have no right to consider one [race] more ape-like than the other."[14] The question of course remains whether Boas, despite the qualifications that he made, successfully convinced a male, white-skinned European and American audience of his skepticism after making such graphic statements about the simian characteristics of Negroes.

Boas's "men of high genius" hypothesis was a pitfall from which he was never able to extricate himself fully, and the tenacity with which Boas held to this conviction demonstrates that one aspect of his views was severely limited by his belief that some racial differences were real. However, even in his own day this hypothesis was proven suspect. Both the anatomist

E. A. Spitzka and the sociologist William I. Thomas pointed out that the brain size of eminent whites varied enormously. Furthermore, Thomas pointed out in 1895 in an article entitled "The Scope and Method of Folk-Psychology" that "functionally . . . [and] the importance of the brain has been unduly emphasized by certain anthropologists. There is far less direct connection between intelligence and brain mass and form than was at the time presumed." While Thomas believed that there was sufficient evidence to conclude "that the cerebral lobes are the seat of consciousness," it was nonetheless true that "the brain is no more essential to intelligence than is the circulation, or digestion, or the liver." According to Thomas, "intelligence is the mediation of action, and all organs and tissues cooperate in forming an association, are equally important with the brain."[15] Although Spitzka and Thomas clearly cast grave doubts on Boas's "men of high genius" hypothesis and science has confirmed their arguments, both men at this juncture were unable to rid themselves of their racial biases and deemed blacks to be intellectually inferior to or temperamentally different from whites, despite evidence to the contrary.

Boas's 1900 address before the American Folklore Society reflected the tension between his liberal humanitarian sentiments and the evidence from physical anthropology. He was willing to pursue the cultural determinist position to some extent. Boas argued that the mind of primitive man differed from that of civilized man not in its organization, as the advocates of the comparative method had proposed, but rather in the character of experience to which it was exposed. The mental functions—abstraction, inhibition, and choice—were all found among primitive peoples; thus, there was no justification for the Spencerian argument that primitive peoples occupied a lower evolutionary stage. In the same address, however, Boas retreated to the argument of black inferiority when he confessed: "A number of anatomical facts [such cranial sizes] point to the conclusion that the races of Africa, Australia, and Melanesia are to a certain extent inferior to Asia, America, and Europe." Nonetheless, Boas argued that there was "no satisfactory evidence" available on whether differences in the size of the brains were "accompanied by difference in structure."[16]

Boas's ambivalences concerning black capabilities were also extended to his discussion of their psychology. He admitted that the descriptive psychological evidence, on which Edward B. Tylor and Herbert Spencer based their generalizations about primitive peoples, had suggested that nonwhites were more fickle and passionate and less original than whites. To him, such arguments were not convincing "because causes and effects were so closely interwoven that it is impossible to separate them in a satisfactory manner, and we are always liable to interpret as racial characteristics what is only an effect of social surroundings." Even on that issue, however, Boas infused physical anthropological assumptions into psychology and immediately genuflected to reactionary beliefs:

> Based on these considerations, we believe that in the more complicated psychological phenomena no specific differences between the higher and lower races can be found. By this, however, we do not mean to say no differences exist or can be found, only that the method of investigation must be different. It does not seem probable that the minds of races which show variations in their anatomical structure should act in exactly the same manner. Differences of structure must be accompanied by differences of function, physiological as well as psychological, and as we found clear evidence of differences in mental structure between the races, so we must anticipate that differences in mental characteristics will be found.

Then, in a feeble attempt to qualify those statements, Boas once again argued that there were variations in all races:

> As all structural differences are quantitative, we must expect to find mental differences to be of the same description, and we found the variation in structure to overlap, so that many forms are common to individuals of all races, so we may expect that many individuals will not differ to their faculty, while a statistical inquiry embracing the whole race would reveal certain differences.[17]

Boas Grudgingly Changes

Nevertheless, between 1894 and 1915, the increasing migration of blacks from the rural areas in the southeastern states to New York City stimulated Boas to take part in reformist activities centering on the condition of the black migrants and compelled him to modify his views concerning the capabilities of blacks. Between 1890 and 1910, the black population of New York City almost tripled. In 1910 there were 91,709 blacks in Manhattan, the Bronx, Queens, Richmond, and Brooklyn. Of that population, 60,534 lived in Manhattan, and 22,708 lived in Brooklyn. "The average Negro migrant," Gilbert Osofsky wrote, "obviously found life harsh and difficult. For those who came, however, conditions in the North did offer a measure of self-respect and the possibility for future advancement that was generally denied the Negro in the South." Nonetheless, the net effect of the black migration was to initiate racial violence and antagonism and exacerbate the "social problems" brought about by urbanization. Although recent studies of African American migrations have attempted to demonstrate that the realities of life in the

North for most southern African Americans were disappointing, I nevertheless concur with many historians' argument that conditions in the North at the turn of the twentieth century were more amenable to black progress because blacks in the urban-industrial North were subject to less blatant forms of discrimination and were able to exercise their voting rights.[18]

Fortunately, Boas was aware of the need to provide a "scientific" opinion on the "Negro problem." He had obtained a position as lecturer at Columbia University in 1896, due to an initial appointment as assistant curator at the American Museum of Natural History by his friend Frederic Ward Putnam, and was tenured in 1899. He joined with Progressives—urban reformers such as Mary White Ovington, Victoria Earle Matthews, Frances A. Kellor, and William Lewis Bulkley, who were concerned with the welfare of African Americans—and searched for order in a city characterized by disorganization and pathological conditions. Boas and Mary White Ovington, one of the founders of the National Association for the Advancement of Colored People (NAACP), were members of the Greenwich House Committee on Social Investigation, a moral reform organization to which other members of the Columbia University faculty belonged, including Edwin R. A. Seligman, Vladimir Simkhovich, Edward T. Devine, Livingston Farrand, Franklin H. Giddings, and Henry R. Seager. Furthermore, Boas published his point of view in the social service magazine *Charities* in 1905, when that magazine devoted an entire issue to the migration of blacks and the subsequent social problems that had arisen as a result of that migration. In addition, Boas penned an article for the first issue of the *Crisis,* the organ of the NAACP, in 1910.[19]

In his article "The Negro and the Demands of Modern Life," which appeared in *Charities* in 1905, Boas apparently tried to resolve the issues he had raised in 1894 when he argued that blacks would produce proportionately fewer "men of high genius" than whites. Although he once again pointed out that the "average" Negro brain was "smaller than that of other races" and that it was "plausible that certain differences of form of brain exist," he nevertheless cautioned that the data did not conclusively demonstrate differences in intellectual ability. Modifying his 1894 position, which had suggested a direct relationship between brain weight and mental ability, Boas argued: "The inference in regard to ability is . . . based on analogy and we must remember that individually the correlation between brain weight and ability is often overshadowed by other causes, and that we find a considerable number of great men with slight brain weight." Although Boas admitted that causes other than brain weight "often" determined mental ability, he was still too committed to physical anthropological assumptions to dismiss those assumptions. Immediately contradicting his statement, which opened up the possibility of "causes" other than brain weight that affected mental ability, he penned a non sequitur: "We may, therefore, expect less average ability and also, on account of probable anatomical differences, somewhat different mental tendencies." Then, in an attempt to minimize the purported differences between the races, Boas brought forth the same argument he had used in 1894: "We may, with the same degree of certainty, expect these differences to be small as compared to the total range of variations found in the human species."[20]

Boas attempted to give a favorable impression of African Americans, despite the measurements indicating that the average cranial cavities of blacks were smaller than those of whites. In a passage that was a direct attack on segregation in the public schools, he wrote:

> There is every reason to believe that the Negro when given the facility and opportunity will be perfectly able to fill the duties of citizenship as well as his white neighbor. It may be that he will not produce as many great men as the white race, and his average achievement will not quite reach the level of the average achievement of the white race, but there will be endless numbers who will do better than the defectives whom we permit to drag down and retard the healthy children of our public schools.[21]

Rhetoric aside, Boas was confronted by an irreconcilable dilemma. As a physical anthropologist, he adhered to the assumptions of his field. The above passage reflects the Boasian paradox that had been part and parcel of Boas's thought since 1894. Insofar as Boas thought the Negro would be "able to fill the duties of citizenship as well as his white neighbor," he was making the case for the full participation of blacks in American life. Yet his formulation of the "approximate" intellectual equality of blacks and whites reflected both his progressive and reactionary values. To the extent that Boas was arguing for the necessity of taking into account individual differences in assessing a person's capabilities—and therefore his or her intrinsic worth in the marketplace—he was making the case for differentiation in the black class structure. However, by suggesting that blacks were only approximately equal to whites, Boas was either consciously or unconsciously providing the rationalization for some discrimination in the economic sector.

Nevertheless, as early as 1905, Boas revealed in his correspondence a healthy skepticism concerning the inferences drawn from the assessments of anthropometric data, basing his objections on the insufficiency of that data. As the series of quotations I will present in this section demonstrate,

Boas always indicated he was an empiricist who had to account for the empirical data he had. Furthermore, he seemed to state constantly that the empirical data were inadequate to support racist conclusions and that they pointed to a lack of support for the argument of black inferiority based on racial difference. Writing to Edward T. Devine, a colleague at Columbia and general secretary of the Charity Organization, in 1905, Boas emphasized "the desirability of collecting more definite information in relation to certain traits of the Negro race that seem of fundamental importance in determining the policy to be pursued towards that race." The problem that Boas thought was paramount concerned "the determination of the period of development of the Negro race as compared to the white race." Proponents of Negro inferiority claimed that there was an "early" intellectual "arrest of development of the Negro child." Boas, who had "gone over available material with some care," found the "evidence is wholly insufficient, and that really the problem must be taken up more." Boas thought that he could "definitely solve our problem" if he could "get a trained observer to collect data on stature, weight, size of head, development of nose, time of eruption of teeth (milk teeth and permanent teeth), puberty and senility." "At the same time," he continued, "I should try to make a test of preliminary cases showing the rapidity of development of practice in Negroes and in whites on some psychological experiment, selecting a test in which influence of school-teaching could count for but little."[22] During this period, as I will show later, Boas thought that psychological testing could provide a definitive statement on the capabilities of blacks compared to whites.

Boas was even more precise about the problems confronting students of race when he contacted Vladimir G. Simkhovich, a colleague at Columbia and member of the Cooperative Social Settlement Society of the City of New York, in 1906 in an attempt to gain monies for anthropometric studies of the Negro.

Among the questions that can readily be taken up are particularly the following.

1. Is there an earlier arrest of mental and physical development in the Negro child, as compared with the white child? And, if so, is this arrest due to social causes or to anatomical and physiological conditions?
2. What is the position of the mulatto child and of the adult mulatto in relation to the two races? Is he an intermediate type, or is there a tendency of reversion towards either race? So that particularly gifted mulattoes have to be considered as reversals of the white race. The question of the physical vigor of the mulatto could be taken up at the same time.[23]

Simkhovich did not fund the project; instead, he referred Boas to other possible sympathetic philanthropists; and in 1906 Boas turned to Felix Adler, a close associate, proposing a museum whose investigation "would have the most important bearing upon the question of a general policy to be pursued in regard to the Negro." "The questions that are obscure," he stated unequivocally, "in reference to this point are innumerable. We do not know the significance of the slightly different type of organization of the brain. We do not know the laws of growth and of development of the negro race; and all these, taken together, should be investigated, and the result of an unbiased, patient investigation of these problems should be of the very greatest help in all practical problems."[24] Boas seemed to be suggesting at this point that physical anthropology had the potential for providing data on the Negro on which public policy should be based.

Although Boas assumed a skeptical posture before white persons who were possible sources of funding for his proposed projects on the anthropometry of the Negro and mulatto, it should be stressed that he held a conviction that most Negroes were inferior to most whites. Expressing this conviction to Reverend James Boddy of Troy, New York, in 1906, Boas asserted: "You may be aware that in my opinion the assumption seems justifiable that on the average the mental capacity of the Negro may be a little less than that of the white, but that the capacities of the bulk of both races are on the same level." Boas admitted that he could "find neither any history nor any anatomical considerations in proof of any considerable inferiority of the Negro race." Always guided by the assumptions of physical anthropology, Boas conjectured that "it seems of course likely that owing to the differences of anatomical traits, mental differences also exist." But he nonetheless concluded "that the differences are slight as compared to the variability found in each race."[25]

It should also be noted that Boas's methodological puritanism also often prevented him from espousing the belief that the equipotentiality of blacks was a scientific fact to blacks who sought his expertise. For example, in response to a paper by R. R. Wright Sr., the African American president of Georgia State Industrial College, which asked Boas to cite "some authorities" that he could "consult upon the ancient history of the African Race, or the Negro in particular," Boas wrote in 1907:

> I think you understand my view in regard to the ability of the Negro quite agrees with what you say in your paper. I wish, however, that it were possible to take up a careful study of this subject, and to present the results to our fellow-citizens in a convincing manner. Unfortunately it does not help us that we ourselves have clear convictions in regard to this subject. The reasons for

> our convictions should be represented in an answerable form, and I believe the only thing that will serve this purpose will be a very painstaking and detailed presentation of the results of studies of African ethnology on the one hand, and of the anatomical features of the central nervous system of the white race and of the Negro race on the other.[26]

In other words, Boas exercised extreme caution in expressing his convictions; he thought the need for further research was a prerequisite for making the case against rigid racial determinism.

Despite his penchant for refusing to express his convictions, in 1909, before reform-minded persons, Boas had begun to minimize the significance of racial intellectual differences between blacks and whites. After reviewing the data on the size of the Negro brain in a short article that appeared in the *Crisis,* Boas stated unequivocally: "The existing differences are differences in kind, not in value. This implies that the biological evidence also does not sustain the view, which is so often proposed that the mental power of the one race is higher than that of the other, although their mental qualities show, presumably differences analogous to the existing anatomical and physiological differences." Boas's thought at this juncture was uneven, however. In the same year he published an article entitled "Race Problems in America" in *Science* in which he stated unequivocally that he believed that there were fundamental differences between whites and blacks:

> I do not believe that the Negro is, in his physical and mental make-up, the same as the European. The anatomical differences are so great that corresponding mental differences are plausible. There may exist differences in character and in the direction of specific aptitudes. There is, however, no proof whatever that these differences signify any appreciable degree of inferiority of the Negro, notwithstanding the slightly inferior size, and perhaps lesser complexity of structure, of his brain; for these racial differences are much less than the range of variation found in either race considered by itself.

Nevertheless, aware of the scientific doubts about physical anthropological explanations of differences in the mental makeup of blacks and whites, Boas wrote in the same article:

> I think we have reason to be ashamed to confess that the scientific study of these [Negro] questions has never received the support either of our government or of any of our great scientific institutions; and it is hard to understand why we are so indifferent towards a question which is of paramount importance to the welfare of our nation. The anatomy of the American Negro is not well known; and, notwithstanding the oft-repeated assertions regarding the hereditary inferiority of the mulatto, we know hardly anything on this subject.

> If his vitality is lower than that of the full-blooded Negro, this may be as much due to social causes as to hereditary causes. Owing to very large numbers of mulattoes in our country, it would not be a difficult matter to investigate the biological aspects of this question thoroughly; and the importance of the problem demands that this should be done.[27]

In 1911, Boas published *The Mind of Primitive Man.* The volume included excerpts from his previously published essays on race, but also contained the most up-to-date data that supported most of the conclusions that Boas had been developing since 1894. It was complete in its refutation of crude racial determinist thinking; complete in its indictment of crude racial prejudice; and cogent in its presentation of the assimilationist arguments.

In 1912, Robert H. Lowie, who had been one of Boas's students, lucidly explicated his mentor's position in reference to the inferences that could be drawn from a critical assessment of the data on "the Negro" emanating from physical anthropology in the *American Journal of Sociology.* "The Negro race may not produce as many minds of exceptional ability as the white race; but so far as its average performance is concerned Boas arrives at the conclusion that there is no evidence for believing in a racial inferiority that would unfit an individual Negro to take his part in modern civilizations."[28]

The Mind of Primitive Man, however, did not mark the culmination of Boas's thought on blacks during the Progressive Era. The end point was not reached until the publication of Boas's foreword to Mary White Ovington's *Half a Man* in 1915. He summed up the view of Boasian anthropology when he stated: "Many students of anthropology recognize that no proof can be given of any material inferiority of the Negro race; that without doubt the bulk of the individuals composing the race are equal in mental aptitude of the bulk of our own people; that, although their hereditary aptitude may lie in slightly different directions, it is very improbable that the majority of individuals composing the white race should possess greater ability than the Negro race."[29]

Boas had, in essence, minimized the significance of purported intellectual differences between blacks and whites insofar as he stressed the fact that the masses of both races were virtually equal. Nonetheless, he raised a key issue that was far from being resolved at his death in 1942. Were the slight differences in "hereditary aptitude" that he detected socially significant? In other words, what were the implications of slight differences in racial aptitudes for the professions and highly skilled trades? Boas could not answer these questions; and they continue to be debated even to this day.

Despite Boas's admission that it was practically impossible to separate the social and hereditary features of the mental makeup of whites and blacks, he had argued in 1894 that "investigations based on physiological psychology and experimental psychology will allow us to treat the problem in a satisfactory manner." "In these and in detailed studies of the anatomy of the central nervous system," Boas suggested strongly, "we must look for a final solution of our problem." In reference to addressing the "psychological problem while excluding such factors," Boas argued that it could be accomplished by investigating "the psychical processes of great numbers of individuals of different races who live under similar conditions." Although that feat had not been accomplished so as "to draw far-reaching conclusions," Boas mentioned

> that two psychologists found differences of favorite colors between children of different races and different ages; that attempts have been made to show that the minds of Negro children cease to develop sooner than those of white children, although the results are not conclusive. Modest investigation of the senses of simpler mental activities of children will give the first satisfactory answer to the important question of the *extent of racial differences* [emphasis mine] of faculty. The schools of our country, particularly those of larger cities, open a vast field for researches of this character.[30]

By the end of the 1910s, the efforts of psychologists to investigate the psychical processes had proliferated. Boas, however, always the methodological puritan, would reject their findings because they lacked methodological rigor. He and his students, including Herskovits, Mead, Montagu, and Klineberg, would become the leaders in the fight against the attempt of psychologists to prove black inferiority on the basis of aptitude tests. It is clear from Lowie's explication of Boas's position that Boas thought—as Frank H. Hankins astutely pointed out in his criticism of the former—"racial differences though real are less extensive and important than popular opinion has heretofore supposed."[31]

Despite the fact that Boas worked within the same essentialist framework as the racists, it should not detract from the subversiveness of his position on the capabilities of African Americans in the context of "the nadir." The initial response to Boas in the field of anthropology was hysterical. In his presidential address to the American Association for the Advancement of Science in 1895, Daniel G. Brinton asserted: "The black, the brown and red races differ anatomically so much from the white, especially in their splanchnic [visceral] organs, that even with equal cerebral capacity, they could never rival the results by equal efforts."[32] Yet, by the early 1900s Boas, due to his security at Columbia and his ties to the Smithsonian Institute, the American Association for the Advancement of Science, and the

American Ethnological Society, had become a powerful figure in American anthropology. His political domination of the discipline resulted in the triumph of his position within that discipline after 1920.[33]

Boas's Influence on African Americans

In the closely allied discipline of sociology, the initial responses to the Boasian position on the capabilities of blacks were determined by the ethnic and sectional backgrounds of the partisans, the extent to which the partisans accepted scientific naturalism as a worldview, and their perception of the social structural changes that were affecting blacks in the nation.[34] By 1918, however, the Boasian position had triumphed. The disciple's leading student of race relations, Robert E. Park, summed up the position of the most prominent sociologists that year when he wrote: "[T]he question remains where Boas left it when he said that the black was little, if any, inferior to the white man in intellectual capacity and in any case, racial as compared with individual differences were small and relatively unimportant."[35] During the next few decades, sociologists would become some of the staunchest supporters of the Boasian position on the capabilities of blacks.

For Du Bois, as well as for Kelly Miller and Monroe N. Work, physical anthropology held the key to the nature of racial differences. All three scholars felt compelled to recontextualize the dominant discourse on race in physical anthropology that was dictated by the pronouncements of Frederick L. Hoffman in his book *Race Traits and Tendencies of the American Negro,* published by the American Economic Association in 1896.

Hoffman, a German-born employee of the Prudential Insurance Company, made the claim that he was "free from personal bias which might have made an impartial treatment of the subject difficult." Nevertheless, the conclusion of the work was an expression of the rampant Darwinism that predicted the impending extinction of African Americans. It was Hoffman's argument that African Americans after the antebellum period were deteriorating physically and morally because of their "race traits and tendencies" rather than because of the adverse conditions to which they had been subjected. For Hoffman, it was "not in the conditions of life but in race and heredity that we find the explanation." Even persons of mixed ancestry were, according to Hoffman, subject to physical and moral deterioration, primarily because "the mixture of the African with the white race has shown to have seriously affected the longevity of the former and left as a heritage to future generations the poison of scrofula, tuberculosis and most of all, of syphilis."[36]

In a thirty-three-page review of Hoffman's work, which was the first publication of the American Negro Academy, Kelly Miller, who had been professor of mathematics at Howard University since 1890, demonstrated that Hoffman reached his conclusion "from a priori considerations" and his "facts have been collected in order to justify it." Miller concluded by arguing: "It is a condition and not a theory that confronts [the African American]."[37]

During the same period, W. E. B. Du Bois was attempting to discredit the myth that suggested that African Americans composed a homogeneous group whose members (except the mulattoes) should be treated alike. While Boas, on the basis of his anthropometric measurements and analysis of the African background of African Americans, was issuing a prescriptive statement—that is, individual merit, not race, should determine a person's position in the American social order—Du Bois was uncovering empirical evidence and offering explanations for the stratification that existed among African Americans in the 1890s. Indeed, the idea of an African American class structure had its origins in American sociology at the turn of the century in the scholarship of Du Bois. The idea, which was a product of the clash between left-liberal and mainstream progressives and Darwinians, has persisted for almost a century as a key analytical concept in social scientific discussion of race relations in the United States. At present, it raises important questions about the relative significance of "race" and "class" as determinants of the status of African Americans, and it is central to the arguments of such distinguished contemporary scholars as Alphonso Pinkney, Thomas Sowell, and William J. Wilson.

Du Bois's idea of an African American class structure had its origins in his attempt to rebut the Darwinian prediction of the impending extinction of African Americans as developed in Hoffman's *Race Traits and Tendencies of the American Negro.* To Du Bois, it was apparent that Hoffman did not have the insight to offer a "proper interpretation of apparently contradictory social facts." Du Bois noted: "If, for instance, we find among American Negroes today, at the very same time, increasing intelligence and increasing crime, increasing wealth and disproportionate poverty, increasing religious and moral activity and high rate of illegitimacy in births, we can no more fasten upon the bad as typifying the general tendency than we can upon the good."[38] Du Bois argued emphatically that Hoffman was incorrect in assuming that such contradictory facts pertained to "the race" rather than to the class structure that had developed since emancipation. Du Bois, in other words, believed that the extent of black progress or retrogression was determined by the individual's rank within the black class structure. At the same time, he was certain that white prejudice was an obvious obstacle to black progress.

Du Bois, whose orientation was a product of both his inferior status as an African American in an Anglo-American-dominated society and his academic training in the United States and Germany, anticipated the work of Robert E. Park and W. Lloyd Warner in the first three decades of the twentieth century. In his 1899 book *The Philadelphia Negro,* Du Bois gathered empirical data that suggested that class differentiation already existed in black America. He wrote: "wide variations in antecedents, wealth, intelligence and general efficiency have already been differentiated with this [African American] group." Despite his emphasis upon differentiation in Philadelphia's major black community, Du Bois brought forth ample evidence suggesting that the attitudes and behavior of the white population "limited and circumscribed" the opportunities of even "the better classes" of African Americans.[39] Thus, for Du Bois, despite the differentiation of the African American class structure, "race" was the most salient variable in American race relations.

For members of the African American, educated elite, the implications of Boas's assessments of the cranial cavities of blacks and whites were revolutionary. For an intellectual like the Harvard-educated W. E. B. Du Bois, Boas's analysis of anthropometric measurements of cranial cavities was truly subversive. Furthermore, on the basis of early data, Du Bois was cognizant of the centrality of physical anthropology as a buttress to the dominant discourse of race in science. As early as 1898, Du Bois, in his article "The Study of the Negro Problem," stated that "anthropological measurement" was one of the four "practical divisions" for "the study of the Negro as a social group." For Du Bois the division included a scientific study of the Negro body. The most obvious peculiarity of the Negro—

> a peculiarity which is a large element in many problems affecting him—is his physical unlikeness to the people with whom he has been brought into contact. This difference is so striking that it has become the basis of a mass of theory, assumption and suggestion which is deep-rooted and yet rests on the flimsiest basis of scientific fact. That there are differences between the white and black races is certain, but just what those differences are is known to none with an approach to accuracy.[40]

Du Bois initiated a relationship with Franz Boas in 1905, a friendship that lasted for more than three decades. In October of that year, Du Bois sent Boas a letter informing him that Atlanta University was planning to conduct a study of the Negro physique for its conference. In the letter Du

Bois sought Boas's expertise in identifying the best and latest works bearing on the anthropology of blacks, particularly their physical measurements, health, and so on. In offering Boas the opportunity, Du Bois indicated that the Atlanta study would be a "great opportunity . . . for physical measurement of the Negro," provided Columbia University would fund the project. In his reply to Du Bois, Boas indicated that he could not refer Du Bois "to anything that is particularly good on the physical anthropology of the Negro." He went on to suggest that he would query Columbia University concerning the possibility of gaining funding for the study of the physical anthropology of blacks.[41] Although Boas did not accept Du Bois's invitation to the Atlanta University conference on May 29, 1906, he did go to Atlanta on May 31, 1906, to speak to an audience made up of black working people, preachers, and professionals on the African background of African Americans rather than about their anthropometric measurement.

In *The Health and Physique of the Negro American,* which was based on the anthropometric measurements of more than one thousand students at Atlanta University, Du Bois in 1906 quoted a memorandum by Monroe N. Work, who was teaching at Savannah State during that year, that took to task scholars, such as Robert B. Bean, who held that the brain of the African American was smaller than that of the Euro-American. Although Work made no reference to Boas (who had refuted Bean's argument the same year), Work concluded:

> The best evidence seems to indicate that the organization and, therefore, the details of the structure of the central nervous system are continually being modified through life. That is, changes are constantly occurring. These changes, which are many and varied, are caused by age, occupation, nutrition, disease, etc. This fact of constant change makes it very doubtful whether any uniformity in the finer details of structure will be found in white brains, particularly if they are brains of different sizes from persons of different ages, statures, etc., and the cause of death not being the same. These facts, in connection with the well established fact that those characters which are said to be distinctive of particular races are found with more or less frequency in other races, seem to indicate that what has been described as being peculiar in the size, shape, and anatomy of the Negro brain is not true of all Negro brains. These same peculiarities can no doubt be found in many white brains and probably have no special connection with the mental capacity of either race.[42]

Du Bois indeed understood the implications of Work and Boas's assessment of anthropometric measurement for the myth of the African American homogeneous group. When speaking to the National Negro Conference, which preceded the initial organization of the NAACP in 1909, Du

Bois asserted that the address of Boas's disciple, Livingston Ferrand, before the conference "left no doubt in the minds of listeners that the whole argument by which Negroes were pronounced absolutely and inevitably inferior to whites was utterly without scientific basis."[43] Du Bois, nevertheless, was uncritical of Boas's reservations about black equality.

Boas's position even influenced the thought of moderate conservatives, such as Booker T. Washington, who were locked in a severe struggle against the forces of racism and reaction in the South. This argument is perhaps best illustrated by the correspondence between T. E. Taylor, a representative of the Sixty-seventh District in the Iowa state legislature, and Booker T. Washington. Taylor wrote Washington in September 1915 concerning a lecture by James K. Vardaman (Mississippi's governor between 1904 and 1908) in Independence, Iowa, in which Vardaman "asserted that the Negro's skull hardens at age of puberty and from that age on there is no mental development." Taylor did not accept the theory. He asked Washington: "What facts can you give me on this point?" In a long response, Washington referred Taylor to the work of Franz Boas and William I. Thomas (a sociologist whose work closely paralleled that of Boas). In the letter signed in Emmett J. Scott's handwriting, the Tuskegeean wrote:

> For discussion of what the best scientists have to say concerning this question I refer you to the recent volume of the Macmillan Company entitled "The Mind of Primitive Man" by Professor Franz Boas of Columbia University, who is, I understand, the leading authority on the question of the mental ability of races. Another interesting discussion of this same subject is by Professor W. I. Thomas of the University of Chicago, in his book on "Sex and Society" in the chapter on "Mind of Woman and the Lower Races." If your public library has the back numbers of the *American Journal of Sociology,* you will find this same article by Professor Thomas published therein sometime during the period 1906–1908.[44]

Like Du Bois, the Tuskegee machine interpreted Boas's position as an attack on the crude racism that did not draw distinctions between the relative abilities of different blacks and stated that all whites were superior to all blacks.

For the Harvard- and Oxford University–educated philosopher Alain LeRoy Locke, Boas's ideas were a point of departure. Locke was an assistant professor of English and instructor in philosophy and education at the Teachers College at Howard University. Paraphrasing Boas, Locke wrote in 1916: "Because of differences [in] anthropological [factors], anthropological points of comparison have now been reduced to such a narrow margin in each instance that the variations between individuals of the same race, and even the same nation, more than outspan the maximum variability between what are regarded as cognate races of mankind." The net effect of Boas's ideas, Locke noted, was to argue that "a really pure science of race is . . . undesirable, not so much because it is impossible, but because even though it were realized, it would be impractical, particularly as contrasted with whatever current practical theories of race are prevailing in society. It could never successfully hope to compete with what men really believe human society to be." Locke concluded: "To the extent, therefore, that any man has race, he has inherited either a favorable or an unfavorable social heredity, which unfortunately is [typically] ascribed to factors which have not produced [it], factors which will in no way determine either the period of those inequalities or their eradication."[45]

Furthermore, Boas influenced members of the African American elite who were not participants in the academy. George Washington Ellis, the Chicago-based attorney and former secretary of the Liberian Legation, in the *Journal of Race Development* (to which he was a frequent contributor), concluded in 1915 that "the ethnological science has been such an influential factor in creating, diffusing and crystallizing race prejudice in the social minds of whites." Nevertheless, the "new ethnology," written by Franz Boas and Alexander Chamberlain (a former student of Boas and the editor of the journal to which Ellis was contributing), in which Ellis believed the truth was being told concerning blacks and whites, asserted that

> physical features, the cephalic angle, the texture of hair, the shape of the head, the color of the skin, the size or shape, or the size and weight of the brain, have *little or nothing* [emphasis mine] to do with the capacity of mind or the moral quality of the soul; that like other race varieties, the Negro is a product of the complex and subtle forces of his milieu . . . acting upon him for centuries past; that there is no naturally superior and inferior race, and that no race has a monopoly on either beauty, intellect or culture.[46]

In short, the African American elite, which, like the participants in the dominant discourse, had conceived of "race" as a supraindividual organic identity, using such terms as racial "essence," racial "genius," and racial "soul," were cognizant of the fact that Boas offered them by far the best deal they were going to get; and they accepted it. The African American elite, who were more biologically assimilated and acculturated than the black masses, accepted Boas's ideas uncritically, primarily because his argument seemed to suggest that caste barriers did not recognize color and class distinctions. The African American elite now had an argument for their acceptance on an individual basis. Thus, despite the fact that Boas's philosophy suggested that proportionally few of them could shape history, it did suggest that there was no basis for the argument that a goodly number should be excluded from participating in society on the basis of equality.

* * *

Despite Boas's adherence to the assumptions of physical anthropology and experimental psychology, he nonetheless knew that whites determined the status of blacks in the American socioeconomic order and that their attitudes and behavior confined blacks to a low position. Thus, during the years between 1894 and 1915, Boas, time and again, identified the racial prejudice of white Americans as the primary determinant of the status of African Americans. He wrote in 1894:

> When, finally, we consider the inferior position held by the Negro race of the United States, who are in the closest contact with modern civilization, we must not forget that the old race-feeling of the inferiority of the colored is as potent as ever and is a formidable obstacle to its advance and progress, not withstanding that schools and universities are open to them. We might rather wonder how much has been accomplished in a short period against heavy odds. It is hardly possible to say what would become of the Negro if he were able to live with the whites on absolutely equal terms.[47]

In 1909, Boas suggested that anthropology had demonstrated "that the impression which we gain from the failure of the American Negro to manifest himself in any of these directions [industry and art] is due, not to native inability, but to the degrading conditions under which he has been placed for generations."[48] In 1911 Boas argued that the purported "traits of the American Negro are adequately explained on the basis of his history and social status." "The tearing-away from the African soil and the consequent complete loss of the old standards of life," Boas argued unequivocally, "which were replaced by the dependency of slavery and by all it entailed, followed by a period of disorganization and by a severe economic struggle against heavy odds, are sufficient to explain the inferiority of the status of the race, without falling back upon the theory of hereditary inferiority." And finally in 1911, Boas argued that white racism was far more insidious than anti-Semitism in the United States. "The Negro of our times carries even more heavily the burden of his racial descent than did the Jew of an earlier period; and the intellectual and moral qualities required to insure success to the Negro are infinitely greater than those demanded from the white, and will be greater, the stricter the segregation of the Negro community." Boas believed white prejudice served an important practical function. He drew an analogy between prejudice and "the old instinct and fear of the connubium of patricians and plebeians, of the European nobility and common people, or of the castes of India." These "emotions and reasoning," Boas suggested, related "particularly to the necessity of maintaining a distinct social status in order to avoid race-mixture." Sociologists, who were the leading authorities on the issue of prejudice, assumed that it was either "instinctive" or in "the mores" and that whites especially opposed racial intermixture because they identified racial solidarity with cultural solidarity. Although Boas argued that white prejudice was "not a physiological dislike," as proven by the existence of a large "mulatto population," it was nevertheless, as the sociologists had argued, "an expression of social conditions that are so deeply ingrained . . . that they assume a strong emotional value." Boas concluded that although laws might "retard the influx of white blood considerably, they cannot hinder the gradual progress of intermixture."[49]

In his article "The Problem of the American Negro," which was published in the 1921 *Yale Quarterly Review,* Boas attacked racists by criticizing their interpretations of anthropometric data. After reviewing the findings of physical anthropologists on the Negro, he did not draw invidious distinctions between blacks and whites. Moreover, his "men of high genius" hypothesis was conspicuously absent. He willingly admitted "that, on the average, the brain of the negro is slightly smaller than the brain of the European." Yet his inferences suggested the possibility of functional similarities: "The response on the part of brains," Boas surmised, "of different structure and size to the demands of life may be very much the same." Furthermore, Boas was critical of some of the psychological experiments. Early in his career Boas had believed that experimental psychology would provide definitive insights on the issue of racial mental differences. He discovered (after twenty-seven years), however, that the investigations into the mental abilities of black and white children were biased. Boas wrote: "I am not convinced that the results that have been obtained are significant in regard to racial ability as a whole. The variability of the results is also very marked and there is an overlapping of racial traits." He was intent on pushing the liberal environmentalist argument as far as possible. Responding to a study by M. R. Trabue, which was based on the culturally biased Army Alpha and Beta tests, Boas argued that northern blacks were not inherently superior to southern blacks. He asserted that it was not true that only "the gifted Southern Negroes emigrated." In a lucid passage he argued that prejudice adversely affected test results:

> [I]n the absence of sound proof this [inherent intellectual] superiority may just as well be explained by the assumption that Northern negroes are exposed to a wider range of experience than Southern negroes. Anyone who knows the abject fear of the Southern negroes who are put under the control of an unknown white officer in foreign surroundings, anyone who knows the limitations of early childhood and general upbringing of negroes in the South, will accept these findings, but will decline to accept them as a convincing proof of the hereditary inferiority of the negro race.

To prove that cultural factors were more significant for an understanding of the plight of African Americans than the study of heredity, Boas, as he had since 1906, turned to a discussion of African achievements to demonstrate that the traits of African Americans were not racial traits. According to him, Africans had made achievements that were essential to world civilization.[50]

Another article that demonstrated that Boas's evolving thought on race was maturing is "What Is Race," which appeared in the *Nation* in 1925. In that piece he sought to delimit the boundaries of the nature-versus-nurture controversy. He mentioned blacks only once; yet the implications for the discussion of the so-called Negro problem were clear. Unlike his pre-1920 writings, Boas argued it was wrongheaded to try to "judge" an individual "by the size of his brain" or by his physiological or mental functions, mainly because those forms and functions "vary enormously in each race, and many features that are found in one race are also found belonging to other races." Indeed, it was "impossible to speak of hereditary racial characteristics because the traits characterizing any individual occur in a number of human races." Although Boas believed that there were obvious differences in the appearance and behavior of certain "social groups," this did not "imply that these characteristics are hereditarily determined." It was obvious to him that "racial strains, when subject to the same social environment, develop the same functional tendencies." When addressing himself to the controversial issue of racial mental differences, Boas pointed out correctly that the "occurrence of hereditary mental traits that belong to a particular race has never been proved." Thus, for him, it was safe to infer that the "behavior of an individual is therefore not determined by his racial affiliations, but by the character of his ancestry and his cultural environment." One could only "judge the mental characteristics of families and individuals, but not of races."[51]

It would be an overstatement, however, to assert that Boas completely rid himself of racist anthropological assumptions. When *Anthropology and Modern Life* was published, Boas was appalled at the literature that had been written that was "based on the assumption that each race has its own mental character determining its cultural or social behavior." Boas stated unequivocally that the concept of racial types was "based on subjective experience." There were "no pure races." Nevertheless, Boas still argued that

> the distribution of individuals and of family lines in the various races differs. When we select among the Europeans a group with large brains, their frequency will be relatively high, while among the Negroes the frequency of occurrence of the corresponding group will be low. If, for instance, there are 50 percent of a European population who have a brain weight of more than, let us say 1,500 grams, there may be only 20 percent of Negroes of the same class. Therefore, 30 percent of the large-brained Europeans cannot be matched by any corresponding group of Negroes.

Defending this practice of comparing the brain sizes of races, Boas thought it was justifiable, as long as "we avoid an application of our results to individuals." The results could not be applied to individuals because "the brain in each race is very variable in size and the overlapping of individuals in the races is marked." "It is not possible," he asserted firmly, "to identify an individual as a Negro or White according to the size and form of the brain, but serially the Negro brain is less extremely human than that of the White."[52] Furthermore, his "men of high genius" hypothesis appeared in the highly revised 1938 edition of *The Mind of Primitive Man.* A captive of nineteenth-century physical anthropology, Boas never quite escaped.

The thought of Franz Boas on blacks, in essence, was paradoxical as late as 1938. He was torn between his commitment to physical anthropological assumptions, which suggested that the races were not equal, and his commitment to cultural anthropology, which suggested that white prejudice was an obvious obstacle to black progress. Furthermore, his study of the material culture and history of the West African ancestors of African Americans was in dynamic equilibrium with his assumption of black physical inferiority. Boas's egalitarian instincts would, however, eventually ascend, for the relentless social structural changes that brought the "social problems" of blacks into visibility after 1900 were exacerbated as more blacks moved to New York City during World War I. Although the social structural changes would have emancipatory implications for blacks after World War II, racism triumphed in anthropology and sociology for another decade and a half. The persistence of racism in disciplines dedicated to determining the laws of human nature give credence to Fredrickson's statement that "history in general does not . . . provide much basis for the notion that passionately held fallacies are destined to collapse because they are in conflict with empirical reality."[53]

* * *

As several historians have noted, during the 1920s and 1930s, Boas and his students—most notably Margaret Mead, Melville J. Herskovits, and Otto Klineberg—were critical of the methodologies of psychologists, such as George Oscar Ferguson, Carl C. Brigham, Joseph Peterson, and Lewis M. Peterson—formulators of the Army Alpha and Beta tests, who used these "intelligence" tests to prove "scientifically" that the vast majority of African Americans were inferior to persons descended from northern and western European peoples. Furthermore, the historian V. P. Franklin has demonstrated that African American psychologists, such as Howard Hale Long, Horace Mann Bond, Herman Canady, Martin D. Jenkins, Joseph St. Clair Price, and Doxey Wilkerson, were skeptical of the claims of Euro-American intelligence testers and published refutations of white psychologists' suspect conclusions during the years between 1923 and 1936.[54]

It is interesting to note that some African American social scientists, in their effort to recontextualize the findings of scientific racists, sought the expertise and support of Franz Boas. In April 1925, Charles S. Johnson, who was the editor of the National Urban League's journal, *Opportunity*, and who would go on to establish himself as one of the country's leading authorities in the field of race relations, wrote Boas concerning an article by Howard Hale Long of the Department of Research of the Washington, D.C., public schools. Johnson wrote that Long's article, which seemed to be "extraordinarily well supported, questions seriously the validity of psychological comparisons of races based upon the current mental tests." Johnson pointed out that Long had "measured and studied thousands of children of different races," and that "his results seem to show that the mental age of white and colored children are not commensurable; that a mental age on the Binet scale for a colored child means more than the same mental age on the same scale for a white child; and that although a colored child might actually have a mental ability, equal to that of a white child, he would nevertheless have a lower mental age." In response, Boas indicated to Johnson in the same month that he was "interested" in reading the paper and asked Johnson to forward him a copy of it.[55]

By 1928, Boas was working on a study of intelligence tests. Abram Harris, one of his former students who went on to establish himself as a leading economist, wrote Boas concerning a meeting that he had with Charles H. Thompson, professor of education at Howard University, who had received his doctorate in psychology at the University of Chicago. "He [Thompson] is interested," Harris wrote, "in making an analysis of cultural factors as they affect the results of mental testing upon Negroes." "I told him," Harris continued, "you are interested in the same thing or something similar to it." Thompson then wrote Boas, indicating that he had spoken with Harris and that Harris had suggested that he write "with the possible idea of effecting some sort of cooperation." Thompson wanted some specific information from Boas. He asked: "Granting the fact that the results of intelligence and educational tests are conditioned by environment, and I think recent investigations show that we must grant this fact—(A) How may this influence be measured, and (B) What are the results of such measurements?" Despite Thompson's query, Boas only indicated he would "be very glad to hear . . . about the work" Thompson was doing.[56]

Boas was willing, however, to reveal some aspects of his project when Howard Hale Long contacted him in 1929. Hale had been informed by Abram Harris that Boas was "preparing some mental tests for pupils with varying cultural backgrounds." "I am quite sure," Long added, "that I do not wholly understand what your program is, but for some time the conclusion has been forcing itself upon me that the current mental tests are not suitable in some respects, for a large number of Negro children." In his reply on March 18, 1929, Boas indicated that he was "trying to get in detail the social background of individual children and during the year . . . intending to work out a psychological test on the basis of this information." Boas did not expect that he could "give any kind of definite information until about the end of the present calendar year."[57]

Whatever happened to Boas's unbiased mental test is a mystery to this writer at this juncture. There are no indications that it was either widely administered to persons of varying social backgrounds or that it demonstrated significantly different results for African Americans. In short, despite his curt replies to African Americans, Boas throughout his career was a source of support for African Americans who wanted to recontextualize the conclusions of the dominant discourse or scientific racism.

In sum, Boas was no racist. He never asserted or advocated that Euro-Americans should maintain a privileged and protected status vis-à-vis African Americans, but on the issue of the defective status his statements were ambiguous. Though harboring doubts about the eventual achievement of a biracial egalitarian society, Boas did not view the supposed defective ancestry of African Americans as sufficiently significant to justify the exclusion of them from the community of scholars or from citizenship in the nation-state. Thus, despite the confines of his period, Boas was a prisoner there to a lesser extent than most other white scholars.

Some space should also be devoted to the relationship of Boas to the

Harlem Renaissance. Boas influenced significantly the graphic artists, folklorists, writers, and critics of the Renaissance in numerous and diverse ways. First, his physical anthropological critique of racial formalism based on the overlapping of the size of the cranial cavities of blacks and whites, which led many to believe that biological race differences were negligible, convinced the leading architect of the "New Negro Movement," Alain LeRoy Locke, to argue, as stated earlier, in 1916 that racial inequalities were to be explained "in terms of historical, economic, and social factors," not in terms of biological factors. W. E. B. Du Bois, one of the leading custodial figures, concurred with this argument, observing that *all* blacks were not intellectually inferior to *all* whites. And Zora Neale Hurston and Melville J. Herskovits tested Boas's conclusions by measuring the headforms of black Harlemites. Charles Spurgeon Johnson, a leading patron of the "New Negroes," drew on Boas's advice directly by corresponding with "Papa Franz" in reference to the relative reliability of intelligence tests. Furthermore, Boas opened the *Journal of American Folk-Lore*'s pages, which he edited, to black amateur folklorists such as Alain LeRoy Locke, Arthur A. Shomburg, Zora Neale Hurston, Arthur H. Fauset, and Carter G. Woodson. Boas, however, began to eschew those black writers' attempts to promote "race consciousness" and to promote his own students instead.[58]

Second, of even greater significance, however, were Boas's revelations about the achievements of black Americans' Western and Central African ancestors. His investigations into the African background and culture, which were published in numerous journals of anthropology and popular magazines between the years 1904 and 1909, paid particular attention to Africa's peoples, their early successes at smelting iron, their artistic industries, and their agriculture, cultures, laws, and state-building, and had already convinced such notable black thinkers during the first decade of the twentieth century, such as W. E. B. Du Bois, Booker T. Washington, Monroe Nathan Work, and George Washington Ellis, that blacks were not the descendants of inferior stocks of peoples. In addition, the disciplined, classical graphic and cultural traditions in black African art that Boas introduced to Americans had a profound influence on Alain LeRoy Locke, who in turn exposed the works to black American painters and sculptors such as Richmond Barthé and Aaron Douglas.[59]

Third, in addition to his erstwhile support of the forays of black folklorists into the field, Boas's financial and institutional support of the "New Negroes" was made possible through the beneficence of Carter G. Woodson, founder and head of the Association for the Study of Negro Life and History. Boas was successful in securing funds from Woodson for Zora Neale

Hurston and the future economist Abram L. Harris. Although Boas blocked the funding of a project by Alain LeRoy Locke on African art in 1926, he nevertheless earlier had provided Locke with the institutional support of the American Association of University Professors when Locke was fired by Howard University's president in 1925.[60]

During the Harlem Renaissance, Boas maintained a gargantuan reputation among both black and white intellectuals—men and women alike. Affectionately referred to as "Papa Franz" by Zora Neale Hurston, Boas was the mentor of Melville J. Herskovits—a major contributor to Alain LeRoy Locke's manifesto anthology *The New Negro*—as well as noted future cultural anthropologists, such as Ruth Benedict and Margaret Mead.[61] These scholars would contribute to Boas's legacy as the father of Americanist anthropology, which was characterized by its revulsion against racism and its advocacy of cultural relativism.

It should be noted also that Boas's advocacy of cultural relativism has fared less well under critique than his antiracist stance. Nathan I. Huggins has implied that many black creative artists admired Boas's relativistic stance on his research on Africa and its cultures and that Boas contributed to the primitivism and exoticism that pervaded much of the Renaissance's outpourings.[62] In reference to Boas's subsequent withdrawal of his support from the black amateur folklorists, Lee D. Baker has noted that Boas, who equated attempts to promote racial solidarity with nationalism, opposed them.[63]

The controversies that have recently surrounded Boas's contribution to the Harlem Renaissance should not detract from his stature. Limited by the state of knowledge of blacks' character and capabilities, his finding in the fields of human difference were nevertheless far more forward-looking than those of the vast majority of his contemporaries. As a consequence, the black intelligentsia seized upon his findings as a means to demonstrate unequivocally that they were perfectly capable of producing great art and criticism. Thus, although some of Boas's findings that they appropriated were used to rationalize the creation of primitive and exotic sensational work, Boas was not to blame. Whatever successes the Harlem artists enjoyed were no doubt directly related to Boas's prodigious efforts.

3 A Gifted Amateur: The Case of George Washington Ellis

In the fall of 1980, St. Clair Drake, the distinguished anthropologist of African American ancestry, published an article in *Black Scholar* entitled "Anthropology and the Black Experience." This adumbration of the history of black Western practitioners of anthropology in the nineteenth and twentieth centuries is significant.[1] It foreshadowed some of the most pressing concerns in the history of anthropology's confrontation with the issue of race. Indeed, recent writings in the history of anthropology on race are, to a large extent, indebted to Drake.

Drake's argument that in the nineteenth century "Egyptology was on the cutting edge of the fight against racism" deserves attention, if for no other reason than its spawning of what Wilson J. Moses calls Egyptocentrism—that is, the process of assigning traditional American racial constructs to the peoples of ancient Egypt.[2] African Americans' fascination with Egyptology as an antidote to European and European American scholars' racism has been documented in recent books by historians such as Stephen Howe's *Afrocentrism* (1998), Wilson J. Moses' *Afrotopia* (1998) and *Creative Conflict in African American Thought* (2004), Mia Bay's *The White Image in the Black Mind* (2000), and Maghan Keita's *Race and the Writing of History* (2001).

At that historical juncture Drake gave minimal attention to Egyptology. He was far more intrigued by the ethnological and ethnographic writings of black Westerners who studied West Africa's peoples and cultures, such as Martin R. Delany, Edward Wilmot Blyden, George Washington Ellis, and William Shepard.[3]

In recent years, several scholars have documented the valiant effort on the part of black Westerners—varying as widely as the Haitian ethnologist Anténor Firmin to the United States–born missionary Alexander Crummell—to subvert the propaganda of European and European American scholars.

Fortunately, according to Drake, Franz Boas emerged at the end of the nineteenth century and engendered a shift in the discourse in reference to the character and capabilities of blacks in both Africa and the West. Boas's well-deserved historical reputation has been thoroughly documented in the scholarly literature, and his place in what the distinguished historian of anthropology George W. Stocking Jr. calls the "hegemonic anthropological traditions" is secure. Nevertheless, Stocking, who has dedicated most of his career to examining "hegemonic anthropological traditions," admits that rescuing "neglected and precursors of paradigmatic alternatives once lost and now to be regained" is a significant endeavor.[4] The thrust of this chapter, which focuses on George Washington Ellis, is to invigorate the aforementioned mission.

George Washington Ellis was not of the historical stature of Franz Boas or his first generation of students, yet he was truly a gifted amateur anthropologist whose thoughts and actions were of great significance to both his contemporaries and posterity.[5] During the early twentieth century, Ellis's ethnographic work on the Vai peoples of Liberia attracted the attention of Franz Boas, W. E. B. Du Bois, and Robert E. Park. Furthermore, scholars writing since 1980, such as St. Clair Drake, Peter Duignan, L. H. Gann, John Brown Childs, and John Hope Franklin have rediscovered Ellis's writings and noted his contributions to both African American thought and the anthropology of his day.[6] Ellis's historical and contemporary significance stems, for the most part, from his fecund yet paradoxical worldview, which had its origins in American anthropology and sociology, American social Christianity, and the African American church. At this time Franz Boas and his first students, along with the University of Chicago sociologist William I. Thomas, had successfully undermined the cultural evolutionists' paradigm and replaced it with the historical particularist paradigm. Nevertheless, Ellis's loyalties were divided between the old ethnological science, which conceived of race as a supraindividual organic entity, and the "new ethnology" of Boas, which argued that there "is no naturally superior and inferior race."

Furthermore, Ellis also exhibited divided loyalties in reference to the claims of some of the white proponents of American social Christianity. Although Ellis disagreed with those social gospel prophets who held that Africa was a place where blacks indulged in moral turpitude, he nevertheless was convinced that Christianity was far superior to all other religions. In addition, African American Christianity—Ellis belonged to the African Methodist Episcopal Church and served as a member of its general financial board from 1912 until 1916—engendered a further split in his loyalties. On the one hand, Ellis embraced a type of universalistic civilizationism, which argued that although nineteenth-century Europe most closely approximated the quintessences of Christianity and civilization, blacks nevertheless were perfectly capable not only of reaching comparable levels but also surpassing them. On the other hand, Ellis preached a type of "romantic racialism" that stressed the inherent superiority of the Negro "soul."[7] Nevertheless, Ellis made a valiant though unsuccessful attempt to shift his theoretical perspective from cultural evolutionism to historical particularism. In so doing, he made a strong case for a shift of the discourse from one that emphasized African barbarism to one that repudiated the idea of African inferiority.

There are no book-length scholarly treatments of Ellis. And despite the existence of a cache of correspondence, diaries, and unpublished articles located at the Chicago Historical Society, the materials on his life before 1905 are scanty. As a consequence, we have but a bare outline of his life and accomplishments before he reached thirty years of age. We do know, however, that he was born to George Ellis and Amanda Jane Trace in Weston, Platte County, Missouri, in 1875.[8] He left his hometown after completing elementary school because it did not provide sufficient educational opportunities and went to Kansas City, Missouri. Although he found greater opportunities in that city, Ellis found that he was "under the pressure of prejudice" and migrated to Atchison, Kansas, where he completed high school in 1891.[9] He went on to law school at the University of Kansas that same year and was awarded the L.L.B. at that institution in 1893. While pursuing his B.A. at Kansas, he practiced law in order to defray his expenses and was active in Republican politics in Kansas. Variously referred to in Kansas newspapers as "eloquent," "the bright and brilliant attorney," "an eloquent colored orator," and "an able exponent of the currency question," Ellis was selected as one of the debaters in the McKinley Club and treasurer of his class at Kansas.[10] After completing his B.A. in 1897, he migrated to New York City and took courses at the Gunton Institute of Economics and Sociology. In 1899, as a result of his activities as a Republican speaker and his scores on a federal examination, Ellis was appointed to the Census Division of the Department of the Interior in Washington, D.C. While working in Washington, Ellis found time to enroll in courses in philosophy and psychology in the School of Pedagogy at Howard University and to participate in an investigation that resulted in a work compiled and edited by Andrew F. Hilyer entitled *Colored Washington.* Furthermore, Ellis, whom one newspaper described "as one of the most efficient and popular clerks in the Census Office," caught the attention of President Theodore Roosevelt and was appointed secretary of the United States Delegation in the Republic of Liberia.[11] As a result of his investigations of the numerous and diverse tribes in the interior during his tenure in Liberia between 1902 and 1910, his reports significantly shaped the State Department's policies toward Liberia.[12] In addition, Ellis completed a significant ethnographic study that was sympathetic to the Vai-speaking peoples of Liberia—the only sub-Saharan African peoples of this period who had developed an orthography—which, after numerous years of rejections by publishers, was brought out by the Neale Publishing Company in 1914. Entitled *Negro Culture in West Africa,* the work marked the end of the tortuous path that Ellis had taken from a position on sub-Saharan Africa that was similar to that of most white and black Americans at the turn of the century to one that adamantly discredited the pervasive racist mythology; finally he succeeded in replacing that mythology with the idea that Africans were peoples who had made in the past, and were perfectly capable of making in the present and future, achievements that were essential to human progress.

After only three years in Liberia, Ellis espoused an anthropo-geographical determinist position, believing, like Joseph A. Tillinghast, that "tropical nature is wont to sustain the idle and the indolent without the dint of labor." Then, assuming, as most of the proponents of neo-Lamarckianism did, that a group's aptitude for achievement was directly affected by the physical environment, Ellis wrote: "The natural effect of climatic conditions is to impair one's desire and ability for intellectual and physical labor." Although Ellis admitted that some of the tribes of Liberia "have men possessed of great knowledge concerning the medicinal qualities of plants, herbs, and roots" and that "the industrial products of the Mandingoes represent a varied use of natural resources and indicate a high order of industrial skill," he nevertheless believed that there were differences in the aptitudes of the various ethnic groups of Liberia. In other words, like white racists, Ellis subordinated individual differences to group differences. "All these tribes," he wrote, possess "different degrees of natural capacity."[13]

In April 1906, Ellis, writing to Otis T. Mason, the head curator of the National Museum in Washington, D.C., still drew crude distinctions between African ethnic groups, mentioning that he found himself "amid a group of peoples of *varied grades of primitive culture* [emphasis mine]." In passing, he stated that he wanted "to try to compare the Vais with the Gora or

Gola-speaking Peoples, a very powerful and warlike people with four tribal varieties."[14]

Perhaps Ellis would have continued to indulge in such stereotypical thinking had it not been for an article by Franz Uri Boas entitled "The Anthropological Position of the Negro," which was published in *Van Norden* magazine in April 1907. After reading the issue in May of that same year, Ellis wrote to Boas:

> To my mind you have stated fairly the position of science as to the ascertained inferiority of Negro peoples and to my mind struck at the very foundation of those erroneous opinions so widely diffused among Caucasian nations, founded upon the supposed conclusions of science, and which have entailed so much injury and injustice upon the darker races. It is a great tribute to any man to announce the truth, but it is a greater tribute to send it forth into a hostile world, when the author must know that it will be received with disfavor and derision by so many millions of his race. But the circle of those who adhere to your views slowly but constantly widens with the processes of the suns.[15]

Ellis went on in this letter to ask Boas to refer him to a publisher or a magazine that would publish his manuscript or installments of his manuscript on the Vai tribes.[16]

Boas, who received Ellis's missive when he returned to New York City from Europe in August 1907, replied, indicating that he was "very much interested in" what Ellis said and went on to state that he would "be very glad if I can help you in the publication of your observations on the natives of West Africa." Boas, who had evinced an interest in the study of Africans, knew that Ellis was challenging stereotypical ideas in reference to those peoples. Boas, however, cautioned Ellis that it was "not quite easy . . . to get material of this kind published." "If you should care to send me a chapter as a sample," Boas suggested, "I could tell you more definitely what can be done." Furthermore, Boas was particularly interested in "a number of special points in the region in which" Ellis was located.[17] Whatever happened to Boas's efforts to get Ellis's manuscript published is unknown.

We know that Ellis was not too discouraged, for he continued his research. In July 1908, he told W. E. B. Du Bois, whom he had met in January 1906 at the African Methodist Church in Washington, D.C., that he had "secured 100 folklore stories and 150 proverbs and prepared a MS of 60,000 words for press in London, Harrison & Sons." Ellis indicated to Du Bois that he was going to visit the "Vai country" during the dry season in order to provide visual material for the manuscript. Ellis's intention at this juncture was to test Jerome Dowd's contention, in volume 1 of *The Negro Races* (1907), which suggested "the view that the study of the Negro Question in American should be begun in Africa." Ellis admitted to Du Bois that he would "not express any opinion as to the correctness of this view"; he only wished to say that he found the "study interesting" and wished that he "had the time, talent and money to work up" his "subject as it should be."[18] Whatever happened to Ellis's negotiations with Harrison & Sons is not known. However, after he returned to the United States and had begun a lucrative legal practice on the south side of Chicago, he began negotiations in December 1912 with the Neale Publishing Company in New York City for the publication of the manuscript on the Vai peoples. After extensive negotiations, in which Walter Neale, the publisher, queried Ellis again and again in reference to the marketability of the manuscript, the Neale Publishing Company brought out Ellis's book, entitled *Negro Culture in West Africa,* in November 1914.[19]

Frederick Starr, a professor of anthropology at the University of Chicago, wrote the introduction to this book. Starr was a seminal figure in American anthropology, primarily because he, as Darnell observes, "was one of the first . . . to work in Africa and the Orient."[20] This proponent of cultural evolution noted that Ellis was the "third colored man to make a conspicuous contribution to the knowledge of conditions and peoples in the Liberian region." The two other African American males to whom Starr referred were Edward W. Blyden and Alexander Crummell. Starr went on to point out that Ellis "deserves a place upon our shelves alongside of the well known books of those [aforementioned] famous men."[21]

Ellis's intentions in this monumental work were not only to discredit previous scholarship by social scientists such as Joseph A. Tillinghast and Jerome Dowd and the contemporary works of social gospel prophets such as James Shepard Dennis, Robert Elliott Speer, Arthur Tappan Pierson, and Frederic Perry Noble but also to replace their racist mythology with an inclusive one. At the outset, Ellis informed his readers that one of his purposes was to help clarify the American race issue, primarily because "the interracial understanding between what is considered the two most divergent and dissimilar ethnic groups" was "largely conditioned upon knowledge possessed of the Negro in Africa." Ellis astutely pointed out that before he went to Liberia much of the information in reference to the Negro in Africa that he had found in encyclopedias, geographies, and works of technologists and anthropologists was "disclosed to be unsupported by the facts." Denying that this image of the Negro in Africa had been intentionally concocted, Ellis argued that "science had hitherto in the main been compelled to rely upon the reports and data supplied by transient travelers and resident visitors who little understood African mentality, institutions and society." Yet, when the European nations partitioned Africa, a group of administrators and "capable resident students"—persons such as Sir Harry H. Johnston, Sir A. B. Ellis, Mary H. Kingsley, Lady Lugard, Dr. J. Scott Keltie, Count de Cardi, E. D. Morel, M. Felix Du Bois, and Dr. Robert H. Nassau—began to present a more realistic depiction of the sub-Saharan African. Nevertheless, Ellis thought it was "more necessary and imperative . . . that the Negro should explain his own culture and interpret his own thought and soul life . . . if the complete truth is to be given to the other races of the earth." Like Boas, Ellis was insistent on emphasizing "the native point of view."[22] In so doing, Ellis felt he was contributing "his proper portion toward the ultimate concord and cooperation of the races in the great upward trend of social progress."[23]

In *Negro Culture in West Africa,* Ellis first took to task those commentators, such as the Wesleyan Academy–trained Vai prince, Thomas E. Beselow, who argued that Vais were of Abyssinian origin. On the basis of the best evidence that he could gather, Ellis concurred with Reverend S. W. Koelle's theory that the Vai people belonged "to the Mande branch of the Negro race," which had "been affected by the same forces that influenced the great Negroland from without and . . . they originated from the Mandingoes in the Hinterland of Liberia." Second, in order to discredit the myth that the majority of Africans could be represented by what ethnologists had described as the "Negro type," Ellis concluded "in personal features that the great majority of Vais afford a flat contradiction to the generally accepted Negro type, although they live under climatic conditions characterized by the most severe and deteriorating influences." Third, Ellis discredited the myths emanating from the work of the historian Joseph A. Tillinghast, which stated that West Africa's climate provided abundant amounts of food, did not force blacks to spend much time cultivating the soil, and did not compel them to develop a high degree of "industrial efficiency." On the basis of his firsthand observation of the Vai people, Ellis concluded that their economic life, "far from being dependent upon natural products, includes cultivation of food materials, the sale of imported articles as well as of the products of their own industrial skill."[24]

In order to refute Tillinghast's contention that West Africans did not inhibit their "sexual proclivities and neglected their youth," Ellis demonstrated that "the Vais live[d] in social groups necessitated by physical conditions, and they maintain[ed] their various secret societies as means by which individuals are governed and prepared for native life. Witchcraft and the social dance [were] important factors in Vai life." Furthermore, Ellis proceeded to refute the contention that blacks were incapable of abstraction by pointing out that "in fundamentals the Vais' language discloses its relationship to the great languages of the world and it is rich and musical in the concords of its sounds." "The written Vai language," Ellis added somewhat chauvinistically, is "a great invention of the Negro brain, original in conception and independent in character."[25]

Ellis saved his most damning criticisms of some of the white commentators for the social gospel prophets. These men depicted sub-Saharan Africa—to use Ralph E. Luker's words—as the locus of "appalling social conditions among Africa's people." It was purportedly a place in which Islam and Christianity vied with one another for the soul of the pagan, indolent, and morally debased sub-Saharan African who reveled in deceit and savagery. And although the social gospel prophets were critical of "imperialist greed," they nevertheless sought to replicate "American Christendom" through the use of African American missionaries in Africa.[26]

Ellis was especially critical of Frederick Perry Noble's assertion in *The Redemption of Africa:* "The Negro is unmoral." After surveying the literature "by competent minds . . . conversant with the dialects and languages of the localities being studied," such as Mary H. Kingsley, A. B. Ellis, M. le Count de Cardi, E. D. Morel, T. J. Alldridge, C. B. Wallis, John Hardford, Caseley Hayford, John Sarbah, and Edward Wilmot Blyden, Ellis concluded: "The quotations from the authorities now extant on the Negro and his life showing that he has not only moral conceptions but moral standards would make a volume."[27]

Yet, Ellis was not a moral relativist. He still carried much of the nineteenth-century African American "civilizationists" ideology intact, for, like Edward Blyden and Alexander Crummell, he was a staunch advocate of the three *Cs*—civilization, Christianity, and commerce—as the most efficient means of redeeming Africa.[28] According to Ellis, the Vai peoples' culture was divided into two elements—the native and the Islamic. The pagan religious life and practice of the Vais, Ellis believed, had certain defects—that is, "superstitions and mysteries"—but this paganism was "still the means" by which they had "sought to find and serve their God." Although respectful of the Vais' form of pantheism, Ellis nevertheless considered Islam, to which he thought 60 percent of the Vais were adherents, was "a vital, living, active force," that stirred "the spiritual nature . . . to its very depths." Ellis believed those Vais "who profess the faith of the Meccan prophet evince a superiority over their pagan tribesman and possess a zeal, dignity, and devotion that at least are impressive."[29] Revealing the racialist deterministic thinking that was endemic to African American and Euro-American thought of the period, Ellis argued the primary reason for the Vais' adherence to the Islamic faith stemmed from the fact that "they are taught that the Negro has an honorable part in the military history and noted achievements of the religion."[30] Furthermore, Ellis noted:

> By the best informed Muhammadans the Africans are made to feel a pride in the fact that their race is recognized in the Koran, which contains a chapter inscribed to a Negro, and that Muhammud was in part descended from an African and had a Negro as a confident [*sic*] in Arabia. It is pointed out that Negroes figured prominently in the progress of Islam, and on one occasion slew a rival of Muhammud. It is said that the prophet greatly admired a Negro poet of ant[e]-Islamic times, and regretted that he had never seen him.[31]

Yet, for Ellis, Christianity was far superior to all religions. As early as December 1909, in an address delivered at the Protestant Episcopal church in Monrovia, Liberia, Ellis, after arguing that "no state has ever been able to rise above the conception and character of its god," stated: "Christianity unified . . . two hostile elements, harmonized the freedom of the North with the culture of the South, and started modern Europe upon the construction of the most progressive, the most powerful and the most imposing civilization which has ever attracted the attention and thought of the human race." Thus, "on account of its universal adaptability, its many sidedness, and its all-embracing truth, Christianity is the great religion of the world."[32] Despite the fact that most of the Vais were pagans and Islamic, Ellis believed Christianity, which had first been introduced to them by an American Liberian, Reverend Daniel Ware, in Cape Mount, Liberia, in 1860, was slowly taking hold. Thus, after surveying and assessing the efforts of Christian educators and missionaries among the Vai-speaking peoples, Ellis concluded: "Science, literature, art, philosophy, and Christianity will do for the Vais what they have done for the nations—that is, enable them to utilize their natural resources and actualize their highest social and spiritual destiny." Once "Christianity and Modern Civilization" were given "Vai roots," "the Crescent [Islam] would wane before the Cross."[33]

Ellis accounted for the crescent's previous victories over the cross by pointing out that the Vais objected to the latter because of "its disintegrating influences upon the family and the state, on account of caste distinctions based on race, and on account of the liquor traffic carried on by individuals living among Christian nations." Ellis admitted that Christianity might "tend to disintegrate the Negro family, founded upon polygamy," yet he still felt Christianity "in the truest and best sense . . . is a great integrating and socializing factor among peoples who are prepared to understand and practice Christian principles, and who have not the weaknesses and the prejudices of undeveloped minds." For Ellis, polygamy was "inconsistent with the highest social and spiritual development of mankind." As a consequence, Ellis thought that "the destruction of polygamy in Africa [should] be accompanied by the modern agents for progress and development that are suitable to the peculiarities of African environment."[34]

Ellis also found wanting the objection to Christianity on account of the caste distinctions that it upheld. "It cannot be argued that Christianity favors any such distinctions," Ellis maintained. Although the white race in South Africa and the southern states of America had "naturally confused difference with inferiority," he thought it to be "wise for the Negro in Africa to accept those principles [Christian ones] and furnish the world the example of what the true Christian ought to be." Furthermore, Ellis also believed that the objection to Christianity based on the fact that some persons in Christian countries were engaged in the "liquor traffic" was "unreasonable" because "there are few things so generally opposed by Christians as the liquor habit." Although Ellis admitted that the "liquor traffic" was "a curse to Africa," "just as slavery was in America," he nevertheless felt that "when Christianity and Civilization have wrought sufficient progress among the nations the liquor traffic will be stopped."[35]

On the issue of whether European civilization was harmful to the Vais, Ellis was as adamant in his defense of European civilization as he was for Christianity. Addressing himself to the argument that the Africans in the interior, where African culture held sway, were superior to Africans who lived on the coast and had contact with Europeans, Ellis concurred that the Africans in the interior were superior. Yet, he held that "in all periods of transition the individual suffers but society gains." The problems stemmed from the fact that the African "had too much contact with the evils of civilized nations, and too little contact with their virtues." For Ellis, the difficulty of assimilating the African was the moral obligation of civilized powers toward Africa. "It destroys the power of European Civilization to actualize for the African his highest social destiny," he added.[36]

Finally, Ellis smuggled in an argument for the superiority of the Negro soul and thus completed his Crummelian-Bookerite synthesis by emphasizing the former's assertion of the inherent "spiritual nature" of the Negro and the latter's image of the Negro as a loyal, suffering servant. Ellis wrote:

> The spiritual nature of the Negro has often excited comment. The meekness with which the American Negro endured the cruelties of slavery and his loy-

> alty to the southern people during the rebellion have both been the subjects of comment. The latter has been cited to his credit and it may be that the former can be. The New Zealanders, the American Indians, the natives of Fiji and of the Sandwich Islands before the civilization of the white man have passed or are passing from the stage of action. The American Negro alone seems to increase and develop. It may be that the Negro's life and training in West Africa have been of service to him in the United States of America.[37]

In a somewhat laudatory review of George Washington Ellis's *Negro Culture in West Africa* that was published in the *Crisis* in 1915, the venerable W. E. B. Du Bois praised Ellis's book, writing that the author "showed, as all serious students of African life prove, the high culture and ability of black people."[38] The leading sociologist of race relations, Robert Ezra Park, did not heap on the fulsome praise that characterized Du Bois's statement, noting in a review in the *American Journal of Sociology* in 1915 that the book's title was misleading, insofar as it was but "an intimate study of a single tribe." Nonetheless, Park concurred with Frederick F. Starr's argument that the Vai-speaking people were "fairly representative of the tribes of West Africa."[39] Walter Dyson, who reviewed Ellis's book for Carter G. Woodson's *Journal of Negro History,* wrote:

> This study by Mr. Ellis of the culture of West Africa as represented by the Vai tribe, is valuable both as a document and as a scientific treatment of an important phase of the color problem. As a document it is an additional and convincing piece of evidence of the ability of the Negro to treat scientifically so intricate a problem as the rise, development, and meaning of the social institutions of a people. Easy, yet forceful in style; well documented with footnotes and cross references; amply illustrated with twenty-seven real representations of tools, weapons, musical instruments and other pieces of handiwork; containing incidentally, a good bibliography of the subject; and finally, with conclusions condensed in the last four pages, it is a book excellent in plan and execution.

Dyson concluded that "the study can be read with profit by all friends of mankind."[40]

Although *Negro Culture in West Africa* was virtually ignored for the next four decades, John Hope Franklin noted in his third edition of the classic *From Slavery to Freedom* that Ellis's book "is valuable largely for its discussion of how a Negro group developed its own alphabet and written language."[41] Similarly, in 1980, St. Clair Drake added: "George Washington Ellis wrote one of the first reliable studies of the Vai-speaking people." Peter Duignan and L. H. Gann, both senior fellows of the Hoover Institute, wrote in *The United States and Africa* (1984): "George Ellis is only one example of this newly stimulated interest in black history and culture."[42]

Nevertheless, Ellis's book was a commercial failure. The publisher, Walter Neale, did not hesitate to express his dissatisfaction in 1915. When the publishing company's bindery was destroyed by fire in 1919, Neale canceled the contract of publication and turned over all of the company's rights in the book to Ellis. By that time Ellis was deceased.

During the same period in which he was attempting to publish *Negro Culture in West Africa,* Ellis was appointed contributing editor to the *Journal of Race Development* by Franz Boas's first Ph.D. student, Alexander Chamberlain, and for eight years wrote many articles for that journal. Furthermore, he was appointed assistant corporation counsel of Chicago by Major William Hale Thompson, was active in Progressive Party politics, and lost a race for judge of the municipal court by a narrow margin. Ellis was, in essence, truly a gifted amateur ethnographer.

Two years before his death, Ellis published a poorly written vanity novel entitled *The Leopard's Claw.* Replete with stereotypes of Europeans, Euro-Americans, and West Africans, it marked a retreat from his attempt to create an unbiased depiction of West Africans in the interior. Emphasizing the fetishes, cannibalism, lying, and deceit of Africans in the interior, *The Leopard's Claw* was a portrayal of sub-Saharan Africa that resembles the myths of some of the social gospel prophets. The only redeeming people of West African ancestry in the entire novel are those who are loyal servants of the English protagonists. Thus, despite his other attempts in the popular media to correct the erroneous impressions of West Africa that permeated American society, in the end Ellis succumbed to the pressures of that society.

PART II

Between Universalism and Particularism

4 The Internalist-Externalist Controversy in the History of Racial Thought

In December 1946, E. Franklin Frazier presented a paper to the American Sociological Society entitled "Sociological Theory and Race Relations." After surveying the writings of sociologists published between 1896 and 1945, Frazier, the first African American to serve as president of a national academic association, concluded that most of the sociological theories that appeared during that period "were merely rationalizations of the existing racial situations." Frazier argued that the ascendancy of the assimilationist orientation in post–World War II sociology was due to the emergence of "a sociological theory of race relations . . . formulated independent of existing public opinion and current attitudes." Frazier had completed his graduate training at the famed Department of Sociology at the University of Chicago; thus it is not surprising that he attributed to his former mentor, Robert E. Park, a monumental role in the development of sociological theories free of the idea of black racial inferiority. Such a change in theory, Frazier suggested, could not have occurred without the strong social currents emanating from the migration of blacks to "the metropolitan areas of the North," which "destroyed the accommodation that had been achieved to some extent following the racial conflict during and following Reconstruction." Despite his willingness to concede that social structural changes affected race relations, Frazier insisted that "Park was the chief figure in the formulation of this sociological theory which provided the orientation for empirical studies of race relations."[1]

Frazier's explanation of why most sociologists had by the early 1920s discarded theories that rationalized the caste-like social order raises many questions. Most conspicuously absent is the role that anthropology, under the leadership of Franz Boas, played in determining the orientation of many leading professional sociologists. Nevertheless, Frazier's hypothesis of the role of the black migration in the formation of theories of race relations is certainly perceptive, and his thesis on that issue has been expanded in works by this author.[2]

Most contemporary scholars who examine the history of the triumph of liberal environmentalism in the American social sciences during the years 1895 to 1945 argue that it was the "internal" developments within the social sciences that generated the movement from racial determinism to cultural determinism. Furthermore, they argue that Franz Boas played the most significant role in the intellectual revolt against racism in the American social sciences.

Typical of the pioneering works that tend to stress the rational aspects of the nature-versus-nurture debate and to assume that Boas possessed a superior intellect that enabled him to undermine the validity of racist theories is Thomas F. Gossett's *Race: The History of an Idea in America.* Gossett states: "What chiefly happened in the 1920s to set the tide of racism was that one man, Franz Boas, who was an authority in several fields which had been the strongest sources of racism, quietly asked for the proof that race determines mentality and temperament." For Gossett, it was the "illogic of racism" that led to its demise in the American sciences and social sciences. He argues that "racism had developed into such a contradictory mass of the unprovable and the emotional that the serious students eventually recognized that as a source of explanation for mental and temperamental traits of a people it was worthless."[3]

Perhaps the most influential student of Boas's racial thought is George W. Stocking Jr. Adopting some of Thomas Kuhn's ideas on the emergence of new paradigms in the scientific community that appeared in his controversial book *The Structure of Scientific Revolutions* (1962), Stocking has argued, in his often-quoted work *Race, Culture, and Evolution,* that the "internal . . . development within *each* of the social sciences conditioned the movement toward an explanation of human behavior in purely cultural terms." He proceeds to state that "in the long run, it was Boasian anthropology rather than the racialist writers associated with the eugenics movement which was able to speak to Americans as the voice of science on all matters of race, culture, and evolution."[4]

While the "internalist" critique was emerging, an "external" forces argument was growing in the discussion of racial thought. Its proponents agree that internal developments were significant; nevertheless, they argue that those developments were a direct product of social structural changes. In response to Gossett, Leonard Lieberman argued in an article that was originally published in *Phylon* in 1968 that "Gossett's position seems to be that of the historian and humanist: men and ideas make history. The view that must be added concerns the influence of cultural conditions. Boas's ideas could only spread when the social structure was ready. Men make history, but they do not do so immediately."[5]

An important, but overstated, assessment of Boas is the late anthropologist Marvin Harris's analysis in *The Rise of Anthropological Theory* (1968). Insisting that the Boas contribution took place in a period of reaction, Harris wrote:

> The attack on racist theories coincided in the United States with a period of strong democratic counter-currents. Boas was a member of an immigrant minority, who as an individual was obviously unprepared to concede the superiority of the dominant white Anglo-Saxon Protestant intellectual and business elites. Nonetheless, he was no superman; without supporting currents powerfully impelled by the conditions of his adopted social milieu, racism might very well have survived and triumphed in America, as it did in German and Italian anthropology. But the anti-racist counter-currents in the United States were nourished by the vast influx of Poles, Russians, and Italians, whose Catholicism or Judaism was not easily worked up into a master-race complex. The immigrant groups participated in the political and ideological struggle to break the pattern of unrestricted competition, which marks the beginnings of United States welfare capitalism.[6]

The conflict between those who view the emergence of the culture concept as the product of internal changes in the social science disciplines and those who believe that the social structure determined the emergence of the concept has yet to be resolved. The historian Hamilton Cravens has attempted to reconcile the conflict with his suggestion that Boas and his students were both transforming their discipline "into a respected science and profession in America" and fighting against racist currents in the nation. The position is stated clearly by Cravens when he writes:

> The culture idea had obvious implications for the stances men took in the world of politics no less than the world of science. The culture idea was at odds with the notion of "Nordic" superiority, not to mention many other values in WASP culture or the assumptions of "mainstream" middle class progressive ideology. The Boasians were separated from WASP culture; several were immigrants, of Jewish background, or both. If the Boasians had a common political posture, probably it was to the left of mainstream, middle class progressivism; they were not impressed by the progressives' vision of

> a clean, efficient, and mechanistically democratic society. They believed that ethnic tolerance and pluralism were indispensable prerequisites to American democracy.[7]

Cravens's explanation of the culture idea as a product of "marginal" men and women gives some useful insights into why it emerged during a period of ethnic upheaval in the United States. However, he does not explain adequately why sociologists, most of whom were of British ancestry, eventually accepted the culture idea. It is my argument that for sociologists, imbued as they were with the mainstream progressive ideology, the gradual acceptance of the Boasian position on race and race relations had more to do with the problems stemming from the migration of blacks into northern cities than with Boas's stature as an anthropologist. Confronted with the evidence of black progress, the leading sociologists found it exceedingly difficult to reconcile that empirically verifiable evidence with theories of black inferiority.

Put another way, Boas's recontextualization of the empirical data of nineteenth-century anthropology generated internal conceptual stresses on the issue of African Americans' racial capabilities and fostered an interest in the social structural changes that were perceptibly transforming the demographic character of the northern urban and industrial areas in which most sociologists lived and worked. In other words, there was no monocausal relation between the rise of naturalism in post-1910 sociology and the subsequent decline of racist thinking in that discipline. Prior internal conceptual stresses—exacerbated by Boasian anthropology in the years before 1911—and contemporaneous social changes were *necessary,* not to say sufficient, conditions for the development of progressive theories of race and race relations.[8]

5 Booker T. Washington: Mythmaker

On September 18, 1895, Booker T. Washington, the young principal of Tuskegee Normal and Industrial Institute, delivered an address to a mixed audience at the opening of the Atlanta Cotton States and International Exposition. Thirty-nine years old, the Tuskegeean had spent nine years in the peculiar institution of slavery and had witnessed its eventual demise. Washington had also lived through the period when the North attempted to reconstruct the South and had seen the reconciliation between two great sections take place in 1877. Furthermore, he bore witness to the subordination of blacks in the South after Reconstruction. Disfranchisement by amended state constitutions had taken place in Mississippi in 1890 and was taking place in South Carolina at the time of Washington's address in 1895. Through the gradual proliferation of Jim Crow laws, extralegal violence, and the removal of blacks from positions in skilled labor—all aided and abetted by the unethical political climate in the South—whites, at the time of Washington's address, had consolidated their higher-caste positions over blacks.

Although he did not mention any specific names, Washington began by scolding black emigrationists "who depend on bettering their condition in a foreign land," and those militant blacks "who underestimate the importance of cultivating friendly relations with the Southern white man as his next-door neighbor."[1] The ex-slave's interpretation of black history stressed the idea that blacks had been loyal servants "nursing your children, watching by the sick bed of your mothers and fathers, and often following them with tear-dimmed eyes to their graves."[2] Revealing his nativist thought, Washington argued that whites "who look to the incoming of those of foreign birth and strange tongue and habits for the prosperity of the South" had a limited knowledge of the black contribution to southern history.[3] Blacks, "without strikes and labour wars, tilled your fields, cleared your forests, built your railroads and cities, and brought forth treasures from the bowels of the earth, and helped make possible this magnificent representation of the progress of the South."[4]

Despite Washington's emphasis on the monumental role blacks had played in whatever achievements the South made during the antebellum period, he argued that blacks were not prepared for the coming of industrialization. During Reconstruction, Washington asserted, "ignorant and inexperienced" blacks "began at the top instead of at the bottom."[5] For those blacks, "a seat in Congress or the state legislature was more sought than real estate or industrial skill . . . the convention of stump speaking had more attractions than starting a dairy farm or truck garden."[6] In effect, Washington exonerated white southerners of any responsibility for the so-called Negro problem and placed it squarely on the shoulders of blacks. Learning the virtues of common labor, he believed, would yield far more gains than politics. In regard to the role of blacks in the South's economy, he suggested that some would find a place in the professions. For the overwhelming number of blacks, however, Washington asserted: "It is at the bottom of life we must begin, and not at the top."[7] Sociologically speaking, he envisioned a South where there would be great social distance between blacks and whites—"In all things that are purely social we can be as separate as the fingers"—yet considerable intergroup collaboration—"one as the hand in all things essential to mutual progress."[8] Projecting the social Darwinist mindset with its emphasis on the survival of the fittest and a buoyant spirit of optimism, the Tuskegee Wizard argued that African Americans would eventually achieve equality, not by agitation for social equality but by a "severe and constant struggle" in the marketplace.[9]

Historical interpretations implying that Washington's Atlanta Exposition address either soothed the consciences of the Justices of the Supreme Court that legitimized Jim Crow laws in the *Plessy v. Ferguson* case in 1896 or was an expedient strategy have generated heated scholarly debates. Those debates, however, seem irresolvable, especially when the adversaries take into account the virulent racism that pervaded the nation and Washington's surreptitious struggle against the forces of reaction in the South.[10] Regardless of what positions the adversaries assume, Washington's ideas deserve close scrutiny, for Washington was more than a mere "man of action." He was a consummate mythmaker. Washington drew on the major myths of his age in reference to African Americans: African inferiority, the civilizing effects of slavery, the horrors of Reconstruction, and the gradual uplift of the African American masses through industrial education. In weaving these tales sophistically, the Tuskegee Wizard created a political mythology that formed the historical element in his moderate liberal ideology. This mythology eventually infiltrated what the distinguished Boasian anthropologist of Native Americans Alfred L. Kroeber labeled "history": historical anthropology, history proper, and sociology. When "history" eventually discredited Washington's mythology, this thoughtful, reflective man modified some of his myths yet left others intact. This essay is an examination of that process.

* * *

On May 19, 1931, in a lecture before his sociology course entitled "The Negro in America" at the University of Chicago, Robert Ezra Park outlined the social philosophy of Washington. Park, who had served as a ghostwriter for Washington between 1905 and 1913 and was the most distinguished student of race relations in the country, asserted that Washington "really represented" the freedman who wanted to attain first-class citizenship. Unlike the aristocratic W. E. B. Du Bois, who represented the educated blacks and, in the tradition of the abolitionists, appealed to "rights" in the Fourteenth and Fifteenth Amendments of the U. S. Constitution in an attempt to make laws that existed operative, Washington thought that whites believed it was their "right and duty to keep" the African American "in his place."[11] Drawing on the ideas of conservative social Darwinist William Graham Sumner, whose concept of "the mores" encouraged what the late Swedish political economist Gunnar Myrdal called a "laissez-faire, do-nothing" approach to white-black relations, Park argued that Washington knew that the subordination of African Americans "was deep in the mores of the South."[12] Furthermore, Park suggested that Washington "realized and knew" that effective laws "must rest" on mores and customs; and, as a consequence, "in order to make laws operative," both whites and blacks would have to be "reeducated"—"particularly the whites."[13] In other words, by changing the "sound, natural conditions which made the mores what they were," one could "then change the mores."[14] Thus, Washington's philosophy of gradual economic uplift through industrial education was, according to Park, set up to "reeducate" African Americans in the South for a new system of labor, in which, unlike slavery, the black masses were supposed to "find work dignifying . . . a privilege."[15] In reference to the positive aspects of Washington's program for African Americans, Park asserted that the "purpose of Washington's education was to convince [the] negro that he could do things. Start him on *his own*."[16]

Furthermore, according to Park, Washington believed that providing African Americans in the South with an industrial education could provide the impetus for transforming the mores of whites. In *agape*-like terms, Park interpreted Washington's philosophy of community in the following manner: "Washington [was] always saying that both white and black have a community of interest. [Washington] didn't appeal to mores, or law, but to the individual. If [the blacks] don't get justice, it reacts back on the whole community. . . . His appeal [was] that interests of negro and white were alike [and] would lead to laws that protect both alike."[17]

Despite what seemed like a sane social philosophy, it should be stressed that Washington, at the height of his influence, publicly adumbrated the political mythology most frequently promulgated to justify turn-of-the-century race relations in order to rationalize his program of the gradual economic uplift of African Americans in the South through industrial education. In his classic American autobiography, *Up from Slavery*, which sold thirty thousand copies between its initial publication by Doubleday, Page and Company in 1901 and 1903, Washington implied that African Americans were the descendants of barbarous peoples and, as a result, only capable of progress under the Christian and civilizing influences of whites. He then enjoined the themes of African primitiveness and the civilizing effects of slavery when he wrote:

> Then, when we rid ourselves of prejudice, or racial feeling, and look facts in the face, we must acknowledge that, not withstanding the cruelty and moral wrong of slavery, the ten million Negroes inhabiting this country, who themselves or whose ancestors went through the school of American slavery, are in a stronger and more hopeful condition materially, intellectually, morally, and religiously than is true of an equal number of black people in any portion of the globe. This is to such an extent that Negroes in this country, who themselves or whose forefathers went through the school of slavery, are constantly returning to Africa to enlighten those who remain in the fatherland.[18]

Washington's ghostwriter, S. Laing Williams, a prominent African American who practiced law in Chicago, was even more emphatic about the progressiveness of Anglo-Americans and the primitiveness of African blacks when he wrote in a biography of Frederick Douglass in 1907: "The chance or destiny which brought to this land of ours, and placed in the midst of the most progressive and most enlightened race that Christian civilization has produced, some three or four millions of primitive black people from Africa and their descendants, has created one of the most interesting and difficult social problems which any modern people has had to face."[19]

Although Washington's and Williams's statements to the contemporary reader seem to be little more than a rationalization for the status quo in white-black relations, compared with other viewpoints at the time, the men's viewpoints were moderate. Other intellectuals such as General Francis A. Walker, James Bryce, Joseph Le Conte, Eugene Rollin Carson, Joseph A. Tillinghast, Paul B. Barringer, Frederick L. Hoffman, and Walter F. Willcox argued that African Americans were degenerating and predicted that they would become extinct. These spokesmen for black degeneracy, as George M. Fredrickson correctly pointed out, were Darwinians. Fredrickson asserted that it logically followed from their position that "if the blacks were a degenerating race with no future, the problem ceased to be one of how to prepare them for citizenship or even how to make them more productive and useful members of the community. The new prognosis pointed rather to the need to segregate or quarantine a race liable to be a source of contamination and social danger to the white community, as it sank even deeper into the slough of disease, vice, and criminality."[20]

It is true that Washington was a social Darwinist of a sort, insofar as his philosophy was primarily materialistic. Washington, however, did not exclude moral or religious forces in accounting for the evolution of humans. For example, he wrote in *The Negro in the South* in 1909:

> The average white man of America, in passing judgment upon the black race, very often overlooks the fact that geographically and physically the semi-barbarous Negro race has been thrown right down in the centre of the highest civilization that the world knows anything about. Consciously or unconsciously, you compare the Negro's progress with your progress, forgetting when you are doing it, that you are placing a pretty severe test on the members of my race. If, for example, we are compared with the civilization of the Oriental countries, the test would not be so severe. But we have been placed in the midst of a pushing, surging, restless, conquering, successful race of people, and you must acknowledge that when the American white man wants to lead, no other race can go far ahead. In fact, he would have the whole field to himself. The progress of the Negro will be in proportion as they learn to get the material things of this world, consecrate them, and weave them into the service of our Heavenly Father.[21]

In addition to disagreeing with the Darwinians concerning a Supreme Being or purpose in the universe, Washington also disagreed with them on the issue of the potency of human beings' agency or will. His embracement of neo-Lamarckianism suggested that will or purpose was bringing about evolutionary change. In other words, the idea of the inheritance of acquired characteristics suggested that not only bad behavior but also good behavior could be transmitted from one generation to another. Washington used the principle to demonstrate that the purported differences between the races were not permanent. "It is only through struggle and the surmounting of difficulties that races, like individuals," Washington asserted in 1909, "are made strong, powerful, and useful."[22] As early as 1899, Washington clearly drew a distinction between his position and that of those intellectuals who believed in the impending extinction of blacks in *The Future of the American Negro:*

> A few people predicted that freedom would result disastrously to the Negro, as far as numerical increase was concerned; but so far as the census figures have failed to bear out this prediction. . . . It is my opinion that the rate of increase in the future will be still greater than it has been from the close of the war of the Rebellion up to the present time, for the reason that the very sudden changes which took place in the life of the Negro because of his freedom, plunged him into many excesses that were detrimental to his physical well-being.[23]

Although it is clear that Washington drew a distinction between his moderate liberal position and that of the prognosticators of the impending extinction of African Americans, he did cast grave doubts about the viability of Reconstruction. The period of Reconstruction, in Washington's view, was one in which "two ideas were constantly agitating the minds of colored people, or, at least, the minds of the larger part of the race. One of these was the craze for Greek and Latin learning, and the other was a desire to hold office." The fascination of African Americans with such status and power symbols, Washington argued, should have been expected from "a people who had spent generations in slavery and generations before that in the darkest heathenism."[24]

Yet the desires of African Americans to learn the classical languages and to hold political office were not the most serious flaws that Washington detected in the defunct Reconstruction period. Washington's major grievance centered on the maternal relationship between the government and the African American wards of that government. Thus he wrote:

> During the whole of the Reconstruction period our people throughout the South looked to the Federal Government for everything, very much as a child looks to its mother. This was not unnatural. The central government gave them freedom, and the whole Nation had been enriched for more than two centuries by the labour of the Negro. Even as a youth, and later in manhood, I had the feeling that it was cruelly wrong in the central government, at the

> beginning of our freedom, to fail to make provision for the general education of our people in addition to what the states might do, so that the people would be the better prepared for the duties of citizenship.[25]

It would be a mistake to argue that Washington was wholly critical of Reconstruction. In fact, as early as 1899, he wrote in *The Future of the American Negro:* "The period of reconstruction served at least to show the world that with proper preparation and with a sufficient foundation the Negro possesses the elements out of which men of the highest character and usefulness can be developed."[26] Two years later, in *Up from Slavery,* Washington stated emphatically that "not all coloured people who were in office during Reconstruction were unworthy of their positions by any means. Some of them, like the late Senator B. K. Bruce, Governor Pinchback, and many others, were strong, upright, useful men." The problem, according to Washington, was not race but education and experience. Therefore, Washington recommended the disfranchisement of both blacks and whites through the use of property and educational qualifications. These "tests," he suggested, "should be made to apply honestly and squarely to both the white and black races."[27]

In short, Washington in 1901 viewed the vast majority of Africans and African Americans as barbarous underachievers who, in his day, were unable to attain the heights of civilization of Anglo-Americans. His solution to the problems of African Americans was industrial education. Through this "education of the hand, head, and heart"—in other words, by becoming acculturated—Washington believed African Americans could eventually contribute to the markets of the world and become prepared for the exercise of first-class citizenship.

In order to comprehend fully the essence of Washington's philosophy of gradual uplift through industrial education, I think it is necessary to examine the social and intellectual influences that produced the idea that the concept was a positive good and therefore a solution to problems centering on the economic arrangements that differentiated most blacks from most whites in the South. The concept of industrial education had its origins in the educational theories of Europeans such as Pestalozzi and Fellenberg. Yet, despite its European origins, the concept with its emphases on morality, thrift, industry, economic independence, and material success, according to the distinguished historian of African Americans August Meier, took hold in the United States as early as the 1820s.[28] The idea that some youth should acquire a trade or mechanical training later arose during the Negro Convention movement as a result of the exclusion of blacks from the skilled trades. As early as 1831, the Philadelphia convention drew up a plan, stating "that a college be established at New Haven as soon as $20,000 are obtained, and to be on the Manual Labour System, by which in connexion with a scientific education they [Young Men of Colour] may also obtain a useful Mechanical or Agricultural progression."[29] The conventions during the 1830s and 1840s continued to adopt plans for potential manual trade schools—to no avail, however. In fact, at a convention in 1848, a committee of five, including Frederick Douglass, stated that "every blow of the sledge hammer, wielded by a sable arm, is a powerful blow in support of our cause. Every colored mechanic, is by virtue of circumstances an elevator of his race. . . . Trades are important. Whenever a man may be thrown by misfortune, if he has in his hands a useful trade, he is useful to his fellow man, and will be esteemed accordingly."[30]

The fallacious idea that a black man or woman with a useful trade would be esteemed and treated accordingly was sustained from 1860 through the 1890s by the Freedman's Bureau commissioners, missionary schoolteachers, the Methodists, and the American Missionary Association. The latter organization helped to create the most successful agricultural and industrial school for blacks before 1890: Hampton Institute. It was at Hampton under General Samuel Chapman Armstrong, who believed industrial education was a moral force, that Booker T. Washington was trained. In his last address, delivered before the American Missionary Association and the National Council of Congregational Churches in New Haven, Connecticut, on October 25, 1915, Washington celebrated "a transformation" that had been "wrought to my race since the landing at Jamestown and the landing of the last slaves at Mobile!"[31] "This transformation involves," he continued, "growth in numbers, mental awakening, self-support, securing of property, moral and religious development, and adjustment of relations between relations. To what in a single generation are we more indebted for this transformation in the direction of a higher civilization than the American Missionary Association?"[32]

Although, as Meier has astutely pointed out, industrial education could be viewed as either "a means for helping the laboring classes to rise in the world" or "a type of instruction suitable for adjusting them to their social role," it is clear that Washington truly believed it served the former function.[33] Yet, despite Washington's optimism, historical hindsight has demonstrated that Washington sustained a myth with a greater degree of falsity than truth. "The fact remains," wrote C. Vann Woodward in 1951, "that Washington's training school, and the many schools he inspired taught crafts and attitudes more congenial to the pre-machine age than to the twentieth century."[34]

* * *

While it is true that most of Washington's political mythology remained intact throughout his lifetime, his myth of Africans was dynamic, due to growing knowledge of African history and the new ideas of anthropology, sociology, and archaeology. Washington, influenced by Franz Boas, Monroe N. Work, Robert E. Park, and James H. Breasted, was indeed a thoughtful, reflective person who slowly modified some of his views until they conformed to the most recent authoritative findings in the social sciences.

In 1904, Boas contacted Washington. Seeking to diversify the racial composition of students in American anthropology, he requested Booker T. Washington's advice concerning the admission of James Emman Kwegyr Aggrey, a Fanti born on the Gold Coast, to graduate study in anthropology at Columbia University. Of Aggrey, who had received a B.A. at Livingston College in 1902, Boas wrote: "He [Aggrey] is a full-blood negro and so far as I can learn, his standing is such that he will require at least one year of undergraduate work before he can be admitted to university. . . . From what I hear from my colleagues who made his acquaintance at the session of the summer school, he is a very bright man. He is, however, without means, and will require support in order to complete his studies. I do not know whether it would be possible to obtain this support here in the city, but I do not think it is unlikely."[35]

Nevertheless, Boas clearly labored when he considered the dismal career prospects that Aggrey would face once he had satisfactorily completed the requirements for an advanced degree: "I very much hesitate to advise the young man to take up this work, because I fear that it would be very difficult after he has completed his studies to find a place. On the other hand, it might perhaps be possible for him to study for two or three years and to take his degree of master of arts, and then to obtain a position in one of the higher schools established for his race. I feel that the matter is a rather delicate one, and I do not wish to advise the young man or to assist him in beginning a study which may ultimately put him in a most unfortunate position."[36]

At the end of the letter, Boas was extremely pessimistic about the employment prospects of Aggrey and suggested they might be solved through Aggrey's participation in the colonial service of one of the European powers. "It is of course evident that if he developed into a good scientist, he could do excellent work particularly in Africa, which would be of the greatest service to science. This is a consideration which makes me desirous of assisting him. On the other hand, I am very much afraid that it would be almost impossible to find a place for him even in this field. Perhaps by proper application, and if he were the right man, it might be possible to get him into Colonial service of one of the European countries that have colonies in Africa."[37]

Booker T. Washington's response indicates that Boas's liberalism was far too progressive for the leading black spokesman of the period. Washington, who believed blacks needed to enter the practical vocations, told Boas:

> Judging by what you state in your letter and knowing what I do, I can not rid myself of the feeling that the course which he is planning to take will be of little value to him.
>
> At the present time I know of so many cases where young colored men and women would have done well had they thoroughly prepared themselves for teachers, some kind of work in the industries, or in the applied sciences, but instead, they have made the mistake of taking a course that had no practical bearing on the needs of the race; the result being they ended up as hotel-waiters or Pullman car porters.[38]

As Boas would later learn, the Tuskegee Wizard was no man's fool. Although Aggrey went on to receive an M.A. at Livingston College in 1912, a D.D. degree from Hood Theological Seminary, and an M.A. from Columbia University in 1922; became a member of the Phelps-Stokes Committee on Education in Africa during the early 1920s; and eventually served as vice-principal of Achimota Prince of Wales College and School in present-day Ghana, Washington's statements had some basis in empirical reality, especially when one considers the career of Zora Neale Hurston almost three decades later. Hurston's biographer, Robert E. Hemenway, has described how Boas did not hesitate to direct her studies in 1934. But even Boas, who had helped Hurston draw up a plan for the Rosenwald Foundation for her doctoral program, was unable to gain long-term support for her, despite the fact that Hurston was the author of a novel and a book of folklore.[39]

In November 1906 Boas wrote again to Booker T. Washington, seeking to speak with him when he came to the Carl Schurz Memorial Meeting in New York City. Boas indicated that he was "endeavoring to organize certain scientific work on the Negro race which," he believed, would "be of great practical value in modifying the views of our people in regard to the Negro Problem." He was "particularly anxious to bring home to the American people the fact that the African race in its own continent has achieved advancements which have been of importance in the development of civilization of the human race." As a postscript, Boas insisted that he wanted to "talk over the possibilities of practical steps in this direction." The Tuskegee

Wizard did not respond to Boas's letter but would later extend an invitation to him in June 1912 to serve on the executive committee of the International Conference on the Negro.[40]

There are clear indications, nonetheless, that Boas modified Washington's image of Africans because of the influences of his ghostwriters, Robert Ezra Park and Monroe Nathan Work. Park had been assigned to work on Washington's history of the Negro in Africa and America, which would become *The Story of the Negro,* but after Park's attention veered to other urgent tasks and the project languished for two years, the publisher insisted that Alvis Octavious Stafford, a teacher at the Institute for Colored Youth, in Cheyney, Pennsylvania, be given the writing assignment. Work and Park then came in to rescue the project when Stafford's drafts were inadequate.[41]

Some background information on Work is necessary to clarify why he was able to play such a monumental role in writing *The Story of the Negro,* a work—to use Louis R. Harlan's words—"significant for its consciousness of Africa" (for more information on Work, see chapter 7). Work, the son of former slaves, was born in Iredell County, North Carolina, in 1866. He was raised in Cairo, Illinois, and rural Kansas. Like many men who formed the ranks of the early sociologists, he embarked on a ministerial career, joining the African Methodist Episcopal Church. Recalling his career from 1897 until 1903, Work wrote:

> At about this time I was here studying to be a preacher. I was in the Chicago Theological Seminary which was located on the west side. Graham Taylor taught something he called Christian Sociology. It wasn't sociology as you know it today. I started with a study of the Negro in crime in Chicago as a sort of term paper. This was in 1897. Graham Taylor was very much interested in it. When I decided to come to the University of Chicago and study sociology in 1898, I brought this paper with me. After I had done some more work on it, it was published in the American Journal of Sociology for September 1900. I think this was the first article by a Negro published in the Journal. I graduated in 1903 specialising in sociology.[42]

After receiving his master of arts degree from the University of Chicago, Work accepted a position at Georgia State Industrial College in Savannah to be near W. E. B. Du Bois. (Work considered Du Bois, along with himself, Richard R. Wright Jr., and Kelly Miller, "the four originals" [Negroes in the newly formed discipline of sociology].) Work was confident that Du Bois, through his pioneering Atlanta series, held the key to a truly meaningful uplift of blacks. So closely was Work allied to Du Bois that he even joined the short-lived Niagara Movement.

Nevertheless, in 1908 Du Bois's archrival, Booker T. Washington, invited Work to come to the Tuskegee Institute. Work stated that when he came to Tuskegee, many persons who were involved in black uplift were asking questions such as, "What has the Negro accomplished? What can he do? Does it pay to educate him? Morally and physically, is he not deteriorating? Has his emancipation been justified?" He noted that Frederick Hoffman's *Race Traits and Tendencies of the Negro* (1896) "had presented a more or less hopeless view." Furthermore, Work argued, "to the indictment by this publication there was at hand no effective answer." A person who believed that all generalizations about blacks should be based on concrete, universally verifiable data—"You can't argue with facts," as he once put it—Work from 1908 on "was compiling a day by day record of what was taking place with reference to the Negro." "Thus it became possible," he believed, "to answer in a factual manner questions relating to all matters concerning him [the Negro]." As a result of answering questions concerning blacks, Work began to publish a biennial with a worldwide circulation. Entitled *Negro Yearbook,* it was "a standard reference on all matters pertaining to the Race."[43]

Work's fascination with Africa had begun in graduate school while studying under William I. Thomas, a scholar influenced significantly by Franz Boas. Before the publication of *The Story of the Negro* in 1909, Work (who would later become a distinguished Africanist) had published three articles treating Africans in the *Southern Workman.* Furthermore, in *The Story of the Negro,* Work quoted Boas extensively on African culture, society, and industry.[44] In sum, Work was the conduit between Boasian anthropology and the African American intelligentsia.

Robert E. Park also helped to ghostwrite the early chapters of *The Story of the Negro.* Born in Harveyville, Luzerne County, Pennsylvania, in 1864, Park was brought up in Red Wing, Minnesota. Trained under John Dewey, he received his B.A. from the University of Michigan in 1887. The erstwhile newspaper reporter received his M.A. from Harvard in philosophy and Ph.D. from the University of Heidelberg in 1904, studying under the distinguished sociologist Georg Simmel. In 1905, Park became affiliated with the Congo Reform Association and organized the American chapter through the Massachusetts Commission of Justice. In the same year, Park, who was financially insecure, was appointed press secretary for Tuskegee Institute by Booker T. Washington for the sum of $150 per month, "with traveling expenses (railway fare and sleeping car, but not hotel)." In return, Park pledged to give "all that I earn by writing or any other means whatever, whether more or less than $1,800 per year, unless by special arrangement, shall be either turned over to the funds of the school or charged against the $150 per month guaranteed me in this agreement."[45]

So intellectually profitable was the Tuskegee period that Park later wrote: "I probably learned more about human nature and society in the South under Booker Washington than I learned elsewhere in my previous years."[46] Nonetheless, after surveying Park's writings during his Congo Reform Association–Tuskegee Institute period, the sociologist John H. Stanfield has written, "although Park was very aware and concerned about exploitation and control of indigenous African peoples by Europeans, this concern was transformed into an apologetic position when the issue was African Americans in the South." Furthermore, Stanfield states correctly that "although Park described at length the adaptive function of Tuskegee and similar institutions in developing the black masses, he was silent about how the model could be implied in Africa without inflicting the very kind of imposition of control he criticized."[47]

While writing *The Story of the Negro,* Park, the radical reformer, wrote to Washington:

> As introduction on to chapter second I wish you would dictate something about your acquaintance with Africa through books and through persons.
>
> What was the first book aside from a geography you read about Africa or any one who had come from Africa?
>
> Did you ever discover when you were young any one of the books, written before the war, to prove the abilities of the Native African? If so, what impression did they make on you?
>
> What Africans have you known[?] Have you met Dube? Did you know Dr. Edward W. Blyden?
>
> Any personal reminiscences you can give me of these men or anything that connects you directly or indirectly with Africa I can use in the second chapter?
>
> Do you know any of the Liberian people?
>
> Please let me have whatever you can along this line as soon as possible. I got a good story from the Fayette Silk Mills, though we ought to see the proprietor, who is in New York before we write anything.
> I am very truly Robert E. Park.
>
> P.S. Don't you know of some colored man who went out to Africa with high hope of settling there, or of reforming and civilizing the natives and who returned, disenchanted?[48]

In response to Park's first question, the following passage appeared in the first volume of *The Story of the Negro:*

> What I was first able to hear and to learn did not, I confess, take me very far or give me very much satisfaction. In the part of the country in which I lived there were very few of my people who pretended to know very much about Africa. I learned, however, that my mother's people had come, like the white people, from across the water, but from a more distant and more mysterious land, where people lived a different life from ours, had different customs and spoke a different language from that I had learned to speak. Of the long and terrible journey by which my ancestors came from their native home in Africa to take up their life again beside the white man and Indian in the New World, I used to hear many and sinister references, but not until I was a man did I meet any one, among my people, who knew anything definite, either through personal knowledge or through tradition, of the country or the people from whom my people sprang. To most of the slaves the "middle passage," as the journey from the shore of Africa to the shore of America was called, was merely a tradition of a confused and bewildering experience concerning whose horrors they had never heard any definite details. Nothing but the vaguest notions remained, at the time I was a boy, even among the older people in regard to the mother country of my race.[49]
>
> After I began to go to school I had my first opportunity to learn from books something further and more definite about my race in Africa. I cannot say that I received very much encouragement or inspiration from what I learned in this way while I was in school. The books I read told me of a people who roamed naked through the forest like wild beasts, of a people without houses or laws, without chastity or morality, with no family life and fixed habits of industry.
>
> It seems to me now, as I recall my first definite impressions of my race in Africa, that the books I read when I was a boy always put the picture of Africa and African life in an unnecessarily cruel contrast with the pictures of the civilized and highly cultured Europeans and Americans . . . in order to put the lofty position to which the white race has attained in sharper contrast with the lowly condition of a more primitive people, the best among the white people, was contrasted with the worst among the black.[50]

Washington did not respond to Park's second and third questions, but in *The Story of the Negro* he mentioned reading Henry Barth's *Discoveries in North and Central Africa* (1850) in reference to the "intermingling of racial stocks" in Africa. In response to Park's question concerning the Africans he knew, the Wizard named some "pure blood" students who received honors at Tuskegee and prominent "pure" black African Americans such as J. C. Price, Isaiah T. Montgomery, Charles Banks, W. W. Brown, Major

R. R. Moten, and Paul Lawrence Dunbar. He then proceeded to tell a story of a Tuskegee student who was part Bushman and part Hottentot who talked about and even showed pictures that demonstrated that his people were "the victims of circumstances."[51] The last of Park's questions were excluded from *The Story of the Negro.*

By 1909, Washington's conception of Africa changed once again. On April 29, 1909, James H. Breasted, an Egyptologist who taught at the University of Chicago, wrote Washington. Breasted had been born into a Congregationalist family in 1865 in Rockford, Illinois. He had received a B.A. from Northwestern [now called North Central] College in Naperville, Illinois, attended Chicago Theological Seminary and Yale University, and received an M.A. and Ph.D. in Egyptology from the University of Berlin in 1894. The nation's leading Egyptologist, he believed that Ethiopia "long supposed to have been the source of Egyptian art and civilization, actually received its culture from the Egyptians."[52] Nevertheless, he told Washington:

> Since 1905 I have carried out an expedition on the upper, or Nubian Nile which has brought back for the first time, exhaustive copies of all the historical monuments now surviving in that distant country. At the same time the recent discovery of papyrus documents containing translations of the New Testament into the ancient Nubian tongue is enabling us to decipher the hitherto undeciphered inscriptions of the early Nubians. The importance of all this is chiefly: that from these documents when deciphered, we shall be able to put together the only surviving information on the early history of a dark race. Nowhere else in all the world is the early history of a dark race preserved.

Washington replied to Breasted on May 6, 1909, with the astute comment:

> I have noticed one fact . . . which lends a special interest to your discoveries: This is that traditions of the most of the peoples whom I have read, point to a distant place in the direction of ancient Ethiopia as the source from which [African people] received what civilization they still possess. This is true, I think, of the people of the Western Sudan and equally true of the Lake Regions.
>
> Could it be possible that these civilizing influences had their sources in this ancient kingdom to which your article refers?[53]

In short, by the end of the 1900s, Washington's position had moved through three stages. Influenced by nineteenth-century racist conceptions of Africans throughout his childhood and most of his adult life, Washington initially conceived of his African ancestors as primitive barbarians. As he came under the influence of Monroe N. Work, Franz Boas, and Robert E. Park, Washington modified his position to acknowledge the contribution of Africans to world civilization. And finally, influenced by James H. Breasted, he had come to the position taken by nineteenth-century African American nationalists: Ethiopia was the disseminator of knowledge to West Africa.

To conclude, it is tragic that Washington accepted and sustained the other myths of his age to such an extent and for so long. Had he not, his economic vision of the black man in the South as a producer who made the white man dependent on him might have achieved varying degrees of realization.

6 Ulysses G. Weatherly: Anglo-American Moderate

As in anthropology, leading scholars of sociology have responded to the fragmentation of the theoretical tradition of Western sociology. Distinguished sociologist Donald N. Levine has suggested in his history of collective narratives that "perhaps it is time for sociology to recover the robustly ecumenical outlook it evinced when the discipline was being established a century ago and to model, for the world community, a way of resolving the cultural crisis of our time."[1]

Levine's nostalgia for the long-gone days of *purported* successes is also reflected in James B. McKee's argument for the return to a "critically disinterested" sociology of race relations. This return, he believes, would result in the revival of "an older democratic commitment to speak to a larger public that includes and cuts across the conflicting racial identities whose fates are inexorably bound together in the same historical struggles."[2]

Levine's and McKee's apparent aversion to the raucousness of identity politics in the discipline of sociology is regrettable, insofar as it is based on the ahistorical assumption that the first generation of professionals in the field of race were somehow free of the taint of biases in the highly charged ambience in which they constructed theories and conducted research. Suffice it to say, my publications have demonstrated compellingly that in sociology's origins in the United States, these scholars, both northern and southern, both professional and amateur, rationalized "human inequality and suffering as the outcome of the working of natural laws."[3] During a period in which the Anglo-American populace displayed hostile attitudes and exercised blatant forms of discrimination against not only nonwhites but southern and eastern Europeans as well, most of the sociological theories that appeared were, to use E. Franklin Frazier's words, "merely rationalizations of the existing racial situations."[4] Thus, although these "liberal accomodationists" did not embrace doctrines of permanent black inferiority and posited that society was evolving toward higher forms of cooperation, "their thinking," as George M. Fredrickson observed correctly more than thirty years ago, "strengthened the case for segregation."[5] Thus, although the first generation of sociologists might have professed what Levine calls a "robustly ecumenical outlook," their works nevertheless betray an exceedingly narrow *provincialism* on the issues of race and race relations until well after the Boasian revolution. In fact, McKee has argued that some sociologists were "floating between" racial determinism and cultural determinism.[6]

Nevertheless, a question that arises is, What were the implications of a midway position for sociologists' analyses of the social order? This article argues that for Ulysses Grant Weatherly, the intermediate position did not affect his theory of race relations, in which he often substituted an equally virulent cultural stereotype of blacks. Holding tenaciously to the belief in the necessity of the gradual uplift of African Americans, Weatherly even sought to transport these types of libertarian conservative ideas to the United States' foreign policy in the Caribbean.

At the turn of the twentieth century—in the midst of the period referred to infamously as "the nadir"—the migration of African Americans into the Midwest precipitated increasing prejudice and discrimination in public accommodations, housing, and labor. Furthermore, obvious "social problems," such as alcoholism, crime, and pauperism, which were the side effects of prejudice and discrimination, plagued many migrants. In Indiana, the black migration was predominantly from Upper South states such as Kentucky, Tennessee, North Carolina, and Virginia. Most of the African American migrants settled in Marion, Vanderburgh, Clark, and Floyd counties. (All of these counties, except Marion, were in the extreme southern part of the state.) These African Americans migrated primarily to urban centers, and to Indianapolis in particular. In 1890 there were 9,133 blacks in that city; by 1900, the number had increased to 15,931.[7] Furthermore, the African American population in Indiana increased from 57,505 in 1900 to 60,320 in 1910. Commenting on the demographic trends in the northern states in general and prognosticating about their implications for the future of relations between blacks and whites, Ulysses G. Weatherly, professor of sociology at Indiana University, wrote in 1908:

> The migration [of Negroes] to the northern cities is destined to have two important consequences. It will augment the southern negro's unrest under the

> social restraints that are now imposed upon him, and will, by opening an easy road of escape, render him less willing to submit to such restraints. It will also, in certain sections of the North where negroes congregate in numbers, lead to a dislike for the race that is likely to result, as it has already resulted in some cases, in outbreaks of positive hostility.[8]

Who was this sociology professor who recognized that the North had an incipient race problem? Ulysses Grant Weatherly was born in the small Quaker town of West Newton (later incorporated into the city of Indianapolis), Indiana, in 1865. He was of humble origins. His father, William Addison Weatherly, was an uneducated farmer who perhaps could neither read nor write and was not particularly interested in his eleven children's educations; his mother, Lydia Dix, perhaps provided the young Ulysses with encouragement, and her family helped with his schooling. Weatherly prepared for college at Pillsbury Academy and graduated from Colgate University in 1890, winning several prizes for his achievements in Latin and history. In 1891, he began graduate work in history and political science at Cornell University, where he served as Andrew White's literary assistant. Furthermore, he spent the 1893–94 academic year in Europe, traveling in England, Germany, and Austria, and studying in Heidelberg and Leipzig. When he returned to the United States, Cornell awarded him a Ph.D. in history. After teaching at Philadelphia Central College for one year, Weatherly was appointed assistant professor in the Department of History at Indiana University. In 1899, however, he changed departments and was appointed head of the Department of Economics and Social Science, which he directed for thirty-six years. Concentrating his interest in sociology and social work, he received national attention, becoming president of the American Sociological Society in 1923. Furthermore, Weatherly's bibliography consists of more than eighty titles, many of which center on race—an issue on which he was considered one of the leading authorities of his day in the discipline of sociology.[9]

Weatherly had first focused on the so-called Negro problem in a chapel ceremony in January 1903, taking what Thomas D. Clark calls "an optimistic view."[10] Although Weatherly viewed Reconstruction as something that permitted African American suffrage and indulged in "disastrous educational experiments which could never be wholly rectified," he felt Booker T. Washington was working to "correct" the mistake of giving African Americans classical education before they had received an industrial education. The *Daily Student* reported on January 26, 1905, that Weatherly believed that if African Americans were taught "farming, shoemaking, black-smith-ing, and other industries, they would be made into . . . useful and peaceful citizen[s], and it is here that we can hope to find the solution of the race problem." He concluded that "Booker T. Washington is the greatest statesman and civilizer of the age."[11]

* * *

Weatherly was among the articulate mythographers, such as Booker T. Washington, Daniel G. Brinton, and Jerome Dowd, who emerged to tell tales about African Americans that rationalized the virulent racism of Americans of Anglo-American ancestry. The major myths of African inferiority, the civilizing effects of slavery, the horrors of Reconstruction, and the gradual uplift of blacks through industrial education also rationalized the ideology of the members of the moderate elite, like Weatherly, who sought to harmonize race relations during the Progressive Era. In his attempt to interpret the laws of society and human behavior, Weatherly articulated and defined the beliefs and values upon which most educated Anglo-Americans acted on the issues of race. He can be viewed as a mirror of the moderate values and beliefs of educated, middle-class Anglo-American intellectuals in Indiana during the first decade of the twentieth century. It must be noted that compared with that of the Darwinians, their defense of the institution of slavery and the limited progress of African Americans was a moderate position.

The first point of difference between Weatherly and extreme racists centered on whether African Americans had retained their cultural heritage. Unlike the extremely racist southern amateur and professional social scientists like Joseph A. Tillinghast, H. E. Belin, Walter L. Fleming, and Howard W. Odum, who believed African Americans still retained the essential culture of their African brethren, Weatherly believed that the slave was a virtual *tabula rasa,* having brought practically no viable cultural heritage with him from Africa. "On the side of cultural and institutional development of the negro's history," Weatherly wrote in 1908, "was almost a blank until he was brought to America as a slave. Whatever achievement he [the Negro] has since made has been upon models which he has taken from the whites."[12] For Weatherly, African Americans were thoroughly acculturated, and their incipient "distinct race consciousness" was "molded and held in check by "their political identification with this country and with the white man's institutions." Yet, it was a mistake, Weatherly argued in 1911, to "characterize the negroes merely as a passive race." For him, "the negro reflects by imitation the civilization of the society in which he lives. His character in any mixed society depends largely on the social standards others set." He supplied examples of this purported truism, which many of his contemporaries accepted, when he wrote: "In Spanish America he [the Negro] has acquired the taste in dress and the pride bearing of the Castilian. In Haiti [he] is essentially French and in Brazil Portuguese. The impress of France is still on the negroes of Louisiana and the Jamaican negro is unmistakably British."[13]

Weatherly's belief that African Americans were mainly receptors of the behavioral patterns of whites contributed to his acceptance of another moderate-inspired myth: that white northerners instigated the Civil War. Like most moderates, Weatherly's historical interpretation of the causes of the Civil War and its aftermath stressed the North's role in exacerbating southern racial tensions. For him, African Americans had never been primarily responsible for racial conflict, either during slavery or after their emancipation. Rather, they had been the "cause and center of a conflict between two opposing types of sentiment among the whites of the North." Weatherly laid most of the responsibility for the antebellum conflict between the North and South upon "militant abolitionism" that, "by arousing the hot passions of southern whites," gave the slavery controversy a bitterness it would not otherwise have had.[14] Furthermore, Weatherly, like many historians of the period, such as northerner William A. Dunning and his southern students, such as Walter L. Fleming, thought that congressional Reconstruction had been injurious to the self-sufficiency of most African Americans. He thought congressional Reconstruction had been a mistake: "The disastrous period of reconstruction fell with peculiar force on the Negro because, in giving him certain things which seemed of great value, it deprived him of that which he needed most of all—wise guidance and gradual initiation into his new position."[15] In short, Weatherly was an Anglo-American moderate.

Although it is true that Weatherly, like W. E. B. Du Bois, correctly noted that white northerners had no liking of or patience with African Americans, Weatherly was nevertheless contemptuous of racial radicals like Du Bois. When writing an assessment of the First Universal Races Congress, a gathering that treated the problems centered on the contact of races around the world, held at the University of London in late July 1911, Weatherly noted that "in the published volume of papers the name of Booker T. Washington is mentioned but twice (one of which mentions it with implied disapproval)." According to Weatherly, "the Atlanta [University]–Wilberforce [University] aspect of Negro sentiment rather than the Hampton [Institute]–Tuskegee [Institute] aspect came before the Congress, and . . . this was what the Congress seemed to want." Although Weatherly admitted that "Dr. Du Bois made a forceful and a perfectly truthful presentation of the situation as he sees it," the Hoosier still asserted that "if the less tragic half of the story had been told the Congress would have had proper basis upon which to judge rightly the Negro question as it is."[16] In short, whatever Weatherly's personal views of Du Bois might have been, it is clear that he was an ideological opponent of the leading African American intellectual.

At this historical juncture, Weatherly was not only a prejudiced person but also a racialist, as the term is commonly understood. "I confess myself a racialist, though of a chastened kind," he would later admit in 1923.[17] As a "chastened racialist," Weatherly believed African Americans and Euro-Americans differed in somatic character and temperament, yet he wrote in 1910 that "with reference to total mental faculty the degree of difference is not so clearly established." Although he was unwilling to make a strong case for the absence of racial mental differences, he nevertheless followed Franz Boas's lead and commented that it was "probable that some individuals of all races are capable of any level of achievement" and that any "ethnic group as a whole may acquire ability in some lines in which it is now deficient." Influenced by Franz Boas's 1894 address to the American Association for the Advancement of Science, entitled "Human Faculty as Determined by Race," Weatherly paraphrased in a tone of agreement Boas's contention of the capacity of the "darker races" to enter upon the level of civilization occupied by the white races.[18]

Nevertheless, the keystone in the argument defending Jim Crow laws was the identification of a purported nexus between racial solidarity and cultural solidarity—ignoring the permeation of African Americans into virtually every sphere of southern life. Sociologically speaking, Washington envisioned a South where there would be great social distance between blacks and whites: "In all things that are purely social we can be as separate as the fingers." Howard W. Odum was more explicit when he argued in 1910 in *Social and Mental Traits of the Negro* that the white southerner felt "that all forms of equality at bottom are based on at least the possibility of intermarriage, which is an impossible admission." Odum contended that the whole way of life that the white southerner cherished seemed dependent upon the maintenance of a homogeneous communal existence. Describing that attitude, Odum stated: "He that violated it [the social community] is without religion and state. In the keeping of it is the highest culture, religion and conduct; it underlies purity, virtue, traditions, ideals and is also intensified in the social emotions and conduct."[19]

Writing in the *American Journal of Sociology* in 1910, Weatherly argued that "the degree of fecundity in race crossing . . . was generally clearly correlated with the degree of cultural difference between parent stocks." When individuals of widely different levels of culture intermarried, "fecundity and vitality" were lowered because of the "transition to an alien mode of life." Another cause of the "relative sterility of mixed unions" was the absence "of harmony in their intimate matters of personal life." Gathering data for Wackler's study of Christian and Jewish intermarriage in Germany, he pointed out that the average number of offspring in families in which the father was a Christian and the mother Jewish was 1.58, as opposed to 4.35 for Christian families and 4.21 for Jewish families. "The variation," he inferred, "is clearly due to psychological rather than physiological causes." In such mixed unions, he concluded, the partners were unable to enter sympathetically into each other's inner lives, and this bred disappointment and ultimately discord.[20]

In writing about areas where racial intermixing had occurred between blacks and whites, as in Jamaica and the southern states, Weatherly infused both psychological and racial determinist assumptions in an attempt to demonstrate that the half-caste was in a precarious position:

> The consciousness of his [the mulatto's] superiority to the more primitive stock raises a barrier against sympathetic cooperation on that side, while on the side of the dominant race he finds no willingness to grant social equality. If he is not more depraved in morals than either of the parent races he at least has acquired the reputation of being so. Unless the two extremes continue to cross; the mixed breed tends to disappear, either by marrying back into the darker race or by approaching the whites through conscious sexual selection, lighter mates always preferred in successive generations.[21]

White prejudice prevented the amalgamation between mulattoes and whites, Weatherly believed, and, relying on Hoffman's statements on Jamaica and Bruce's research on the South, he thought that the number of mulattoes was declining because they were only able to mix with blacks.[22]

Weatherly's vacillation between attributing the problems of racial intermixture to psychological determinants on the one hand and biological determinants on the other was never satisfactorily resolved. Of particular note is his belief that the normal "ethnic-instinct of self-preservation" prevented intermixture between the vast majority of blacks and whites. The term *ethnic-instinct* was typical of the many loose concepts in turn-of-the-century sociology: it was not clear at this date whether the concept of "instinct" referred to an inborn or an acquired action-pattern. Weatherly, for instance, argued that the "ethnic-instinct" was evoked by the white's "consciousness of long stretches of cultural advance which the darker race is deemed incapable of approximating."[23]

Arguments in favor of the desirability of black and white intermarriage, which Weatherly noted had emerged in the writing of Wendell Phillips in the antebellum abolitionist movement, were still offered by some northern whites. Weatherly, however, discerned a relationship between the size of the black population and the northern white attitudes toward black and white intermarriage. The Hoosier noted that views favoring intermarriage were held "in communities where the Negro never has been found in sufficient numbers to have been the cause of aroused race consciousness." On the other hand, southerners, cognizant of the mass of blacks in their midst, opposed intermarriage because they viewed it as a threat to white society. The insistence on the color line by whites, Weatherly conceded, was "often the outgrowth of prejudice and passions rather than scientific analysis." Despite his worry that prejudice and passion might "become a serious social danger," Weatherly felt such actions could be tolerated. It was obvious to him that "for certain societies and for limited periods it can hardly be disputed that the practical identification of racial solidarity with cultural solidarity furnished a wise principle of social action."[24]

When not dealing explicitly with the polygenist argument (i.e., the argument for the multiple creations of man), Weatherly's and Odum's writings contain a degree of truth—insofar as they correctly describe both northern and southern hostility to intermarriage. Their writings give credence to Gunnar Myrdal's "rank order of discrimination" hypothesis, which suggests: "Highest in this order stands the bar against intermarriage and sexual intercourse involving white women."[25] Neither Washington nor Weatherly—nor Odum—was critical of the prejudice against intermarriage. They seemed to suggest that this prejudice was a natural part of the social order; consequently it was the *right* attitude. By assuming this uncritical stance, they were neglecting what Howard Brotz, a recent sociologist, labeled in 1970 "the theoretically elegant solution to the Negro problem": biological assimilation. It seems clear, despite the variability of race relations in the history of the United States, that as long as blacks remain in the country, the hostility toward black and white intermarriage will persist. Thus biological assimilation, which would absorb the black population, is merely a theoretical solution. Although one might disagree with Weatherly's and Odum's attitudes toward intermarriage, they, at least, did not underestimate the strength of racial prejudice.

* * *

After 1910, Weatherly's positions on the intellectual capabilities of African Americans and the viability of "race mixing" were consistent with his earlier positions. In his only book, entitled *Social Progress* (1926), he wrote: "That racial differences are real is fairly well established despite the frenzied denials of emotional champions of racial equality." But he qualified his position somewhat when he conceded that "until the ethnic explanation of intellectual levels is more thoroughly demonstrated it is safer, as William I. Thomas suggests, to take the individual rather than race as the real variable."[26] In reference to the antiamalgamation argument, Weatherly did not necessarily have to assert that there were intellectual differences between Euro-Americans and African Americans in order to rationalize his biased points of view. Weatherly argued that since social problems arose "from the crossing of highly alien stocks," that was sufficient to justify his position on racial intermixture. Mixed groups, he argued, "vary decisively from the parent kinds and are not adapted to either, for they not only have different physical traits, but cannot claim a definite social status in either group." Although Weatherly did not mention the mulatto specifically, the implication for white-black crosses was perfectly clear, for he stated that "crossbreeds" were "usually unwilling to be classed with the group which has the lower prestige, and are denied admission to full standing with superiors." Furthermore, it was obvious to him that "in psychic type" the crossbreeds were "unstable and often exhibited the worst qualities of both races."[27]

As late as the 1920s, Weatherly was extending the "white man's burden" to the Caribbean, an area in the Americas in which he was considered an expert. In fact, President Calvin Coolidge appointed him an unofficial investigator of conditions in Haiti in 1926 during the United States' military occupation of that republic that had begun in 1915.[28] As late as the mid-1920s, Weatherly was still embracing pre-1910 moderate Anglo-American attitudes in reference to African Americans in the Caribbean. "Were the Negro less easy-going and easy-living he must either have migrated or died out under the stress of this unequal competition," he commented in 1923 in reference to black–East Indian relations in the Caribbean. Nevertheless, Weatherly argued that "the Negro belongs perhaps to the most docile and modifiable of all races" and, thus, "readily takes the tone and color of his social environment, assimilating to the dominant culture with little resistance." As a consequence, he thought the Negro could possibly prosper on islands such as Barbados, Trinidad, Dominica, St. Lucia, and St. Vincent if African Americans on those islands adopted Booker T. Washington's program of gradual uplift through industrial education. Weatherly wrote:

> The Negro is culturally backward because he has a low standard of consumption. Unless his wants are diversified and elevated, the production of more

> wealth would not materially benefit the mass of the population. Education is the agency which is best adapted to change the mode of living; and thus far education in the Lesser Antilles has largely failed to grasp the vital connection between schooling and the needs of practical life. Just as during the post-emancipation period in the United States Negroes conceived of education as a means of escaping commonplace or disagreeable work, so here it is usually looked upon as a release from unpleasant responsibilities. Properly interpreted, vocational education for a backward people is a training in the art of living just as much as in the art of making a living. It will inculcate a spirit of pride and ambition along with an adequate technique in the management of one's affairs at the given time and place. Technical training in agriculture and domestic science is of course necessary where these arts are in such a retarded state; but skill without imagination and constructive economy would not carry the race far. The Negro's unreliability as a laborer and farmer can be corrected only by pressure from within. Diversified wants and a constantly improving standard of living alone can discipline him into habits of steady industry. The ideals upon which Hampton and Tuskegee have worked are those which seem to be peculiarly adapted to and needed by the West Indian populations.[29]

Haiti, however, supposedly presented a special set of obstacles because the French core culture was different. "By temperament and experience less industrial and therefore more congenial to the simpler nature of the African. They had less of race prejudice; they crossed more willing with the blacks; and the color line was less rigid than in English colonies. They also had more gaiety, a keener artistic and dramatic sense and less rigorous moral attitudes." As a result, when the United States took control of the Haitian schools and courts, according to Weatherly, "the influence of a masterful psychic culture of French origin superimposed on an African temperament clashes with a masterful technical efficiency which the Americans have introduced in practical administration." Weatherly went on to predict that when the United States withdrew from Haiti, it "may sink back into something of the old state of lethargy and disorder; but some . . . of the material advantages of the occupation will probably be retained."[30]

In short, even on issues of people of African descent in the Caribbean, Weatherly in the 1920s applied the same stereotypes he had appropriated in reference to African Americans in the United States at the turn of the century. Thus, even in his mature years, he remained a "chastened racialist," a staunch advocate of the Anglo-American moderate position, thereby miring American colonial policy in the Caribbean in a useless formula of African American uplift that had not worked and could not work, even in the United States.

7 A Kind of Conservative: Monroe Nathan Work

The purpose of this chapter is to examine and analyze the life and writings of Monroe Nathan Work, an African American social scientist who was associated at different junctures in his career with both W. E. B. Du Bois and Booker T. Washington. Although overshadowed by the two giants in contemporary scholarship centering on African Americans, Work is truly a significant figure, not simply because he, along with Du Bois, initiated the empirical tradition in American sociology and helped introduce both European and African Americans to the glories of the West and Central African peoples during the medieval period but also because throughout his life, he marshaled empirical data that called into question widely accepted generalizations in reference to personalities, trends, and events that affected African Americans in the United States of America. In so doing, he helped enhance the efforts of great numbers of persons of African descent who were attempting to lead useful, productive lives during the age of Jim Crow.

Furthermore, Work's ideas on race and race relations had their origins in the African American church, American anthropology and sociology, and American social Christianity. As a consequence, Work, like his fellow social gospel prophet Harlan Paul Douglass, saw African Americans—to use the words of Ralph Luker, the distinguished historian of social Christianity—"as persons, persons who should enter the American mainstream to be sure, but persons who made their own contribution to it and thus transformed the model of the good and true American."[1] Indeed, we are indebted to Monroe Nathan Work for paving the way for Martin Luther King Jr.'s composition of the "dream"—a dream that in our time has been appropriated and perverted by both European American and African American conservatives and liberals alike.

Work's worldview that masked his "dream" was truly imbricated, reflecting intellectual, economic, cultural, political, and social stresses that affected Americans in general and African Americans in particular. Between his birth in 1866 and his migration to Chicago at the age of thirty in 1895, Work's subscription to the buoyantly optimistic American success myths—upward mobility through land ownership and/or education—was etched into the attitudes and behavior of many of the freed people. During the same early period of Work's relatively long life, his family background of self-reliance was given even greater stimulus to augment. His family's newly granted mobility, the protonationalism of the African American Episcopal Church, and his success in secondary school, despite his financial hardships, racial discrimination, and age, instilled in Work the values of perseverance and the virtues of the Protestant work ethic. Yet, even during those years, despite his initiative, conduct, character, and work ethic, Work's attempts to fulfill the freed people's dream met with mixed results.

Work, however, persevered after he migrated to Chicago, resisting the temptation to embrace the selfish, secular mythology that was adopted by so many European American and African American elites during the period that has been aptly labeled by August Meier the "Age of Booker T. Washington." Lured to the liberal wing of the social gospel movement during the years between 1895 and 1903, Work, who was pursuing his quest for a postsecondary education, sought also to uplift his less fortunate fellow African Americans—many of whom were recent migrants like himself. Through not only his leadership and participation in the settlement house movement but also his scholarship, Work attempted to bring the social gospel prophets' "Kingdom of God" to earth.

Upon completing his A.M. degree in 1903, Work's engagement with reform through social and political activism (he participated in several African American middle-class, self-help organizations and the 1905 conference of the Niagara Movement) and scholarship in which he began to address cultural issues continued in Savannah, Georgia. Furthermore, in his scholarship he wrestled with the nature-versus-nurture controversy, espousing the ideas of Franz "Uri" Boas in reference to the intellectual equality of whites and blacks and the historical achievements of Africans. For Work, who scrutinized Boas's empirical findings closely, Boas's conclusions were proof that African Americans were capable of progress.

After 1908, Work became a major contributor to Booker T. Washington's uplift ideology propaganda, emphasizing African American self-reliance and capacity for progress, which, George M. Fredrickson has noted correctly, "contradicted white supremacist ideology."[2] In short, Work did not adhere to the selfish, secular mythology that characterized the espoused ideologies of many of his fellow American thinkers.[3] Nevertheless, after Washington's death, Work held on to many of the conservative views of the former. He believed that African Americans did not favor repeal of the disfranchisement laws, provided those laws on the book were impartially enforced. Furthermore, during the 1920s and 1930s, he stressed the progress of African Americans and downplayed problems that were a result of racism. Work died in 1945 at a time when his brand of libertarian conservatism was being severely tested.

The Early Years: 1866–95

During the years between 1890 and 1900, approximately 185,000 southern blacks migrated from their native region, primarily to urban-industrial centers in the Northeast and Midwest. At the beginning of the decade, *some* of the migrants were "a self-selecting population," insofar as many of this group were generally both more highly educated and financially stable than most blacks in their indigenous region.[4] In Chicago, for example, where blacks in 1900 numbered only 30,150 out of a total population of 1,698,575—or approximately 1.8 percent of the city's population—this group of migrants included many prominent members, among them the antilynching crusader Ida Wells-Barnett and Jesse Max Barber, editor of the magazine *Voice of the Negro*.[5] Like many of the other "talented tenth" migrants, both of them came to Chicago in order to escape the racial pogroms in the South. Although Wells and Barber were members of elite black circles, the vast majority of blacks who followed in their tracks during the latter half of the 1890s were dirt-poor farmers and laborers.[6]

Work did not fit neatly into either of the two aforementioned categories. He was born in Iredell County, North Carolina, in 1866 to Alexander and Eliza (Hobbes) Work—both of whom had been emancipated the previous year. Yet, despite the ratification of the Thirteenth Amendment in 1865, which was supposed to end involuntary servitude in the United States, true freedom for the former slaves in the South in general and in North Carolina in particular had yet to be attained at the time of Monroe's birth. The enactment of the Black Codes, which with the support of the courts effectively suppressed agricultural wages and bound the freed people to unfair labor contracts, had enabled large landholders to relegate the ex-slaves to the status of a servile workforce. Furthermore, a drought had occurred in the Piedmont area in 1866, reducing agricultural production in Iredell County and resulting in an intolerable situation for the freed people, as well as for some of their white counterparts.[7]

It was within this context that Alexander Work temporarily left his family in 1866 in order to join the small but steady stream of ex-slaves who migrated from the rural South to the North during Reconstruction. (African Americans' migration, Robert Higgs has observed, acted as a "safety valve," insofar as it limited exploitation to which they could be subjected.)[8] Yet, unlike many of the freed people—most of whom migrated to large urban areas—Alexander moved to Cairo, Illinois. In reference to Cairo, English journalist Edward Dicey commented in 1865: "When the universe was allotted out between heaven, earth, and hell, there was one allotment intended for the third department, and crowded by mistake into the second; and to this topographical error Cairo [owed] its . . . existence."[9] The remark was certainly a hyperbole.[10] For the elder Work, Cairo was a city in which he earned enough money while laboring as a tenant farmer to send for his family the next year. Alexander displayed this type of initiative again ten years later when he left Cairo and migrated to and later brought his family to Sumner County, Kansas. With hopes of becoming an independent farmer, Alexander acquired 160 acres and raised wheat, oats, and corn, and thereby gained a relative degree of prosperity. Alexander was typical of those freed people who were called "Exodusters"—persons who sought to raise their socioeconomic status by cultivating land in Kansas that had been acquired as a result of the Preemption Act and the Homestead Act. For Monroe, who completed his elementary education and then supported "an invalid father and an ill mother" until his mother's death in 1889, the route to advancement would not be through farming (although he tried his hand at it several times) but through education.[11] Nevertheless, the elder Work had in all probability taught Monroe the importance of perseverance and initiative in the face of obstacles—a lesson he would later teach to African American youth.

Monroe's quest for social advancement through education began in 1889, when at the age of twenty-three he enrolled in high school in Arkansas City, Kansas, and, while working several odd jobs, came under the influence of David Ross Boyd (who would later become president of the University of Oklahoma). Under Boyd's tutelage, he graduated from high school in 1892 at the age of twenty-six, ranking as the best mathematician in the history of the school.[12] Work's strengths in mathematics would provide him with the foundations for his future use of descriptive statistics that would distinguish his empirical worldview from the armchair theorizing of distinguished sociologists such as Franklin H. Giddings, Albion W. Small, Lester F. Ward, and Edward A. Ross.

A man of tenacious initiative, Work desired further education, which could only be obtained by accumulating funds that would be saved from his remuneration for work. After one term of teaching at a private school in the Creek and Cherokee Indian territory (teaching, preaching, and menial jobs were virtually the only professional fields open to educated African Americans at that time), Work embarked on a career in the ministry. The reasons behind this decision are not known. We do know, however, that he was ordained a pastor in the African Methodist Episcopal (AME) Church in the fall of 1892 and became the pastor of a congregation in Wellington, Kansas, the same year. The AME Church at the time of Work's entrance into the pastorate had a long and illustrious history. Founded in 1794 by Richard Allen and Absalom Jones, the AME Church, until the middle of the nineteenth century, lacked a strong central hierarchy, "a situation," which James T. Campbell argues, "ensured that ministers were responsive to the concerns of their congregates." The AME Church hierarchy, as Campbell has pointed out, was, however, intent on refuting the stereotypes that blacks were naturally slavish and could not govern themselves.[13] The AME Church hierarchy was conservative on the issue of race. George M. Fredrickson has pointed out correctly that AME Church leaders argued that the primary obstacle to the solution of the American race problem was not European American prejudice. (They viewed prejudice as superficial, not as "a deeply ingrained attitude.") As a consequence, these African American men insisted on the dire need of the African American masses who composed their church to adopt the culture of middle-class Anglo-Americans. "Through their upright behavior and internalization of the Protestant work ethic," Fredrickson has suggested, AME Church leaders believed that the African American masses could demonstrate that they "were qualified to exercise all the rights of citizenship."[14] In short, AME Church leaders, insofar as they attempted to preserve and transmit the values of the Anglo-American core culture through separatist means, were typical of nineteenth-century African American middle-class nationalists.[15]

Thus, under the leadership of Bishop Daniel Alexander Payne, after 1852 the AME hierarchy sought to improve the ministry, music, and modes of worship in the churches.[16] The attempt to upgrade the modes of worship had dire consequences for Work, primarily because he was naturally restrained in his sermonic style—it was said "his lips barely moved when speaking." We do know that after less than one year, Work's congregation was critical of his reserved rhetorical style and terminated his appointment.[17] Nevertheless, Work did not immediately abandon his desire to become a clergyman who preached middle-class Anglo-American conformity. Only when he was introduced to the newly emerging academic discipline of sociology in Chicago did he begin to realize that in order to bring the "Kingdom of God" to earth, he must dedicate himself to help in solving the problems confronting African Americans in his midst. In so doing, Work sought to counter the unscientific and slipshod generalizations that were being made in reference to the etiology of their low socioeconomic status in the American social order.

After his dismissal from his pastorate, Work pursued the first dream of his father's generation—land ownership—as a means to further his education. Work was able to acquire eight acres of land when the federal government opened up Cherokee lands in Perry, Oklahoma. He farmed there until 1894. Following a long illness and a job in which he delivered cattle to meat-packing houses in Chicago, Work was appointed to a teaching job in Kay County, Oklahoma, for which the Board of Education ruled that he should be paid the equivalent of those teachers who had received a "second grade certificate," despite the fact that he had attained the highest score on the mathematics test. As a consequence, by 1895, Work was convinced that he needed more education in order to obtain suitable employment. He migrated to Chicago in the same year.[18] It was only fitting that in Chicago, Work would eventually attempt to help uplift African Americans whose major "social problems" stemmed from the pangs attendant to migrating to and living in a city wracked by uncontrolled industrialization and unprecedented population growth.

Indeed, during his early years, Work embraced a relatively conservative social ideology that would eventually permeate nearly every aspect of all of his scholarly works. Work was typical of those African American leaders who legitimated the social and economic policies of the dominant white elites who defended social hierarchies "based on character, education, and property through honest effort." Persons like Work viewed it as their task to elevate the masses not through radical social and economic policies but through social control—that is, by inculcating African American with the proper feelings and understanding of their predicament.[19]

To sum up, during his early years, Work subscribed to the masses of ex-slaves' Reconstruction versions of the American success myths, which the historians August Meier and Kevin K. Gaines have described as upward mobility through land ownership and/or education. Drawing on his superior skills in mathematics during the next nine years, Work would investigate through his scholarship the etiology of criminal behavior on the part of

African Americans in Chicago, the history and contemporaneous state of African American property ownership in the city, and the state of the African American ministry in midwestern states.

In these investigations, Work would address himself to Fredrick L. Hoffman's argument that African Americans were "degenerating." Work would argue, on the basis of his statistical data, that an "excess of crime among the Negroes" was due to the transitional state of African Americans from slavery to freedom. Furthermore, he would draw on his statistics to demonstrate convincingly that African Americans in Chicago had made progress in property ownership and in improving their churches. In short, beneath the imbricated layers of his statistics, Work's values can be exhumed: his antiracism, his belief in the necessity of cultural assimilation, and his faith in the importance of African American uplift through intragroup self-help and solidarity. The aforementioned values gradually surfaced in his scholarly writings in Chicago.

When Work migrated to Chicago in 1895, his aspiration for more education was manifest. In the same year, he enrolled in the Chicago Theological Seminary—the foremost Congregational school of theology in the Midwest. At the seminary, Work took courses from William Graham Taylor, a liberal Christian who had left a flourishing social ministry in Hartford, Connecticut, and a professorship at the famed Hartford Theological Seminary in order to accept a chair and head the first "Department of Christian Sociology" in the United States.[20] Taylor was a proponent of the social gospel movement—a liberal, Christian movement that, as the recent historian Ralph E. Luker has noted, sought "a fresh application of the insights of the Christian faith to pressing problems of social order that gained widespread circulation" among turn-of-the-century religious reformers.[21]

Yet, unlike many social gospel prophets, such as the conservative Joseph Cook, whose primary concern was with the ethics and practices of capitalism, Taylor, who would be Work's seminal influence on such matters, was, like the progressive social gospel prophet Washington Gladden, primarily concerned with such social facts as crime, the family, immigration, race, and housing. Taylor's liberal, Christian outlook, in short, suggested that the individual was to be saved—not in the other world but in his or her social context. Taylor's emphasis on the necessity of changing the customs of society in order that the individual would reach his or her potential implied that society, not the individual, dictated the conditions under which persons lived.[22]

Although the extent to which Taylor's voluntarism and environmentalism affected Work's thinking at this time is unknown, we do know that Work wrote a paper on the crime perpetrated by African Americans in the city of Chicago. That paper was the genesis of an article that Work would publish in the *American Journal of Sociology* in 1900—the first piece by an African American to appear in that scholarly journal. By that time, Work, who had graduated from the seminary, had entered the University of Chicago to study sociology. Although he would later disclose that he had transferred his career from the ministry to sociology because he thought "a theological education was not a very good education, being too limited in extent," the reasons behind the change were far more complex.[23] The complexity of Work's decision stemmed from the emergence of a type of sociological positivism that reinforced his fundamentally sound, empirical worldview, his associations with proponents—both African Americans and European American—of the social gospel who allowed him to partake in the effort to solve the "social problems" that overwhelmed many citizens of Chicago, and his intense revulsion against the brand of social Darwinist determinism promulgated most explicitly in the writing of Frederick L. Hoffman.

Work and Empiricism

Like so many clergymen who formed the ranks of early sociologists, Work would seek—to use his biographer Linda O. McMurry's words—"to test the power of the social gospel."[24] In other words, Work would utilize empiricism—induction from the observed facts—for the purpose of his moral struggles.[25] "If sociology," Work wrote in articles that revealed his penchant for a morally corrective empiricism, "has primarily to do with human beings in their associative capacities, then its primary function is through investigation and research to collect a body of information that will point out, make clear, what those relationships are and what in the present, the now, should be done in order that these relationships may be more harmonious, more just, and proper."[26] By embracing an empirical worldview, many Christian reformers—or, to be more precise, reformers who were Christians—believed that morality would manifest itself once the social sciences presented the facts about culture, society, and human behavior. Even freethinkers such as W. E. B. Du Bois thought social scientific scholarship would supply the public with "a body of information" that would "be a safe guide for all efforts toward the solution of the many Negro problems" of major urban-industrial areas.[27] Although persons such as Work and Du Bois were mistaken in their notion that when more European Americans learned more about African Americans they would no longer be prejudiced and in so doing would shape prudential public policies, they were not mistaken about the importance of a body of social scientific knowledge.

Work and the Social Gospel in Black and White

Work's responses to "social problems" in Chicago were shaped not only by his advocacy of the use of empirical data to aid the case for reform but also by his embrace of African American Christianity. At the turn of the twentieth century, African American Christianity exhibited a type of universalistic civilizationism, which asserted that nineteenth-century Europe most closely approximated the quintessences of Christianity and civilization. Blacks nevertheless were not only perfectly capable of reaching comparable levels but also surpassing them. On the other hand, African American Christianity also asserted a type of "romantic racialism" that stressed the supposed inherent superiority of the Negro "soul."[28] At various points in his career, Work expressed either or both of these positions. In an attempt to put theory into practice, Taylor founded Chicago Commons Settlement House, an Institutional church that supplemented preaching, prayer meetings, Sunday School, and pastoral visitation with activities such as adult education, clubs, and social groups. He also was an associate of prominent reformers such as Clarence Darrow, Bishop Fallows, Reverend Frank Gaunsalus, Robert Ingersoll, Shailler Matthews, Mary McDowell, and Reverdy Ransom.[29]

During this period in Chicago, when Work met two influential African Americans who would become significant figures in the AME Church hierarchy, Reverdy Ransom and Richard R. Wright Jr., he espoused the universalistic variant of African American Christianity—primarily because of his allegiance to Ransom. Ransom, who viewed himself in the tradition of abolitionists such as John Greenleaf Whittier and William Lloyd Garrison, was an AME minister (and later bishop) and had attended both Wilberforce College and Oberlin College, receiving his bachelor of divinity degree from Wilberforce in 1886. After several pastorates in small midwestern towns, he was appointed pastor of Bethel Church in Chicago and worked with Jane Addams in the social settlement Hull House. With help from Addams, Ransom bought the Institutional Church.[30] Under Ransom, Chicago's Institutional Church and Social Settlement became an organization that provided for black migrants from the South as well as black middle-class residents of Chicago.

Like most universalistic civilizationists, Ransom held—although he would later embrace a variant of romantic racialism—that African Americans were primarily responsible for their won "elevation." Thus, the Institutional Church was dedicated not only to such aspects of religious life as sermons, prayers, and songs but also—to use Ransom's words—"the betterment of humanity and for the uplifting of their race." Developing his idea of uplift fully, Ransom stated:

> Not only in its narrower sense is the religious life developed in the Institutional Church, but humanity in all its breadth is taught. With it the duty to the growth of the body, as well as the mind is ever put to men and women, and the boys and girls who take advantage of the privileges of this house. Lectures and talks are of daily occurrence, but while cultivating the minds, these people are reminded that physically, through inheritance and long unhappy environment, that their bodily development is uneven. The men therefore are urged to use the well-equipped gymnasium in the basement of the church, while the women are told of the health, strength and happiness that will surely come from giving an hour or two every week to the class in physical culture.[31]

Work played a prominent role at Ransom's church, managing its club for boys, which met on Fridays. Work's group, the Dearborn Club, whose membership ranged in age from ten to seventeen, included a few whites. "Mr. Work," Ransom noted in his autobiography in 1946, "has been brought to public notice recently by some clever magazine articles pertaining to his own people, but nowhere in life will he ever do more good than among the [Dearborn Club]."[32] Clearly, Work, like Ransom, was dedicated to racial uplift and manhood development. Put more precisely, Work embraced a type of protonationalism in which African Americans would, rather than beseeching white Christians for help, uplift other African Americans.

Of equal significance to Work's development and later career was his relationship with Richard R. Wright Jr. Wright was born in 1878 to Major Richard R. Wright and Lydia Elizabeth (Howard) Wright. The elder Wright, who had entered a missionary school when he had been freed from slavery in Georgia, had received bachelor of arts and master of arts degrees from Atlanta University and went on to become president of Georgia State Industrial College. The younger Wright received a Georgia school education and attended Haines Institute and Georgia State Industrial College; he then moved to Chicago, where he earned bachelor of divinity and master of arts degrees at the University of Chicago. While working on his degrees at Chicago, Wright developed a firm friendship with Work.[33] Work later recalled:

> Richard Wright, junior, was here then and a fellow named Carney and a fellow named Young. We were the only colored students at the University. We would go around to the churches, Wright would read a little Hebrew, I would read a

> little French, Carney some German, and Young some Greek. We formed two debating teams; Wright and myself against Carney and Young. I learned the importance of facts. Wright and I had the facts and we would always get the decisions because the other fellows might say the facts we offered weren't so but they couldn't offer any against them. You can't argue with facts. . . . When we [Wright and Work] were here we talked together and decided the thing to do was to get the facts about the Negro before the country and the way to do it was to study the Negro.[34]

After a year of study in Germany and a year as a pastor of a church in Chicago, Work's debating partner had minored in sociology while pursuing his bachelor of divinity degree at the University of Chicago. Wright later worked with W. E. B. Du Bois on the Atlanta University series. Furthermore, he studied in Germany and then entered the graduate school at the University of Pennsylvania. In 1905 Wright earned a doctorate in sociology. He was the first African American to be awarded the doctorate in sociology in the United States in 1911; he studied under Carl Kelsey. His dissertation, *The Negro in Pennsylvania: A Study in Economic History,* was published in 1912 by the AME Book Concern in Philadelphia. Although Wright's book was a compendium of facts in reference to the debilitating social problems of African Americans, it was while writing his dissertation under Kelsey that Wright began to develop serious reservations about Work's dictum: "You can't argue with the facts." In his bitter disputes with Kelsey, Wright stated unequivocally: "I contended that given the same statistics and the same body of facts, my interpretation of these should be more valid than his [Kelsey's], for I knew what it is to be a Negro-American from experience and he did not."[35] Wright communicated his insider's perspectives years after his debates in Chicago; and whether or not he revealed his feelings in reference to white social scientists who were empiricists and disagreed with their fellow empiricists who were African American is unknown. Wright went on to become, as James T. Campbell calls him, perhaps the "most distinguished of the AME Church's twentieth-century bishops," despite—or perhaps because of—his embrace of romantic racialism. In fact, Wright's romantic racialism would later characterize Work's thinking.

During the same period, when he was developing relationships with key associates, the future social scientist entered the University of Chicago, which had been in existence for a mere eight years, having been founded by the Baptists in 1890. Under its first president, William Rainey Harper, the University of Chicago sought not only to provide both advanced research and graduate training but also to engender a better society. With these aims in mind, Harper recruited fellow Baptist Albion W. Small to establish the department of sociology there. During a twenty-year period between 1892 and 1912, Small appointed several reform-minded evangelical clergymen and descendants of clergymen, such as Charles R. Henderson, Charles Zueblin, George Vincent, and William I. Thomas, the son of a lay Methodist minister. Thomas is the sociologist whom Work said "influenced" him.[36]

Thomas had received a doctorate in English literature from the University of Tennessee and studied literature, folk psychology, and ethnology in Germany. He then pursued graduate study in sociology at the University of Chicago, receiving his doctorate from that institution in 1896. The early writings of Thomas, whose main interests at that time were physical anthropology and social psychology, on the issues of the differences between the races followed the lead of the founder of modern American anthropology, Franz "Uri" Boas. So closely did the arguments of Thomas parallel those of Boas that later sociologists credited him with helping to develop the liberal environmentalist creed. Thus, although Thomas believed that there were differences in "temperament" between the races, he vociferously denied that intellectual differences were substantial.[37]

Work had been at Chicago nearly a year before he met Thomas. "I happened to meet him [Thomas]," Work recalled in 1908, "while looking after a laundry agency I had." "Thomas was living in Graduate Hall [now Blake Hall]. I went to get his laundry and we entered into a conversation." During that previous year, he had taken courses in history of sociology under Albion Small, Charles R. Henderson, and George Vincent. "I saw what Thomas was doing with social origins," Work recalled, "had connection with the study of the Negro. I began taking Thomas' courses."[38]

For Thomas, who, like most scholars of this period, thought blacks were "savages," the study of these peoples was not only "fascinating and important" but also "esoteric." There were two significant factors that compelled Thomas to study savages. First, evolutionary theory suggested to him that "not a single situation in life can be completely understood in its immediate aspects alone. Everything is to be regarded as having an origin and a development, and we cannot afford to overlook the genesis and stages of change." Much to his dismay, social scientists, despite embracing the theory of evolution, failed "to learn from the life of the lower human races"—lessons "even more important than those which they have learned from biology." Second, and perhaps even more important, Thomas argued that "we consider that the human race is one, that human mind is everywhere much the same, and that human practices are everywhere of the same general pattern." In other words, historians have made a serious mistake of ignoring the "institutional life of savage society" and thus have failed to "perceive the significance of the savage for any study of civilization."[39]

Thomas's methodological approach also influenced Work. Thomas's "approach," John Mark Tucker observes, "was detached, scientific, unemotional, and it emphasized the value of concrete, objective studies of human behavior rather than desires to reform society." Although Work did not allow his tutelage under Thomas to influence his reformist concerns, he accepted the latter's methodological approach and his penchant for geographical and historical explanations for the origins of "sentiments, ideas, interests, and beliefs among racial groups rather than racial classificatory schemes.[40] In Thomas's courses, Work wrote papers on the African medicine man, agriculture, music, and the family—works that were published in the *Southern Workman* between 1906 and 1909. It was also under Thomas's mentorship that Work brought his first article to publishable form.[41]

In his article "Crime among the Negroes of Chicago," Work took Frederick L. Hoffman and other Darwinians to task. Hoffman, a German-born employee of the Prudential Insurance Company, was the author of *Race Traits and Tendencies of the American Negro,* published by the American Economic Association in 1896. The work was an expression of the rampant Darwinism that predicted the impending extinction of African Americans. Hoffman argued that African Americans after the antebellum period were deteriorating physically and morally because of their "race traits and tendencies," rather than because of the adverse conditions to which they had been subjected. For Hoffman, it was "not [in] the condition of life but in race and heredity that we find the explanation."[42] In other words, spokesmen for black degeneracy thought that blacks could not be assimilated into the American social order and because of their inferior innate endowments could not compete with whites. As a consequence, they would eventually die out. Southern counterparts, during the same period, to northern spokesmen for black degeneracy and extinction, such as Hoffman, have been described by Joel Williamson as the purveyors of the "radical" mentality—that is, the mentality that considered that African Americans were retrogressing since slavery to their African heritage of bestiality and savagery and that, as a consequence, they would become extinct in America.[43] For both northern Darwinians and southern "radicals," there was "no place" for African Americans in the United States.

Sociologists of African American descent, such as Kelly Miller and W. E. B. Du Bois, who separately reviewed Hoffman's book, attacked his black degeneracy thesis. Kelly Miller, professor of mathematics at Howard University, led the charge to undermine Hoffman in 1897 in a thirty-three-page review of *Race Traits and Tendencies of the American Negro,* in which he concluded that Hoffman's assertions were based on "a priori considerations." Furthermore, Miller argued that Hoffman's "facts have been collected in order to justify . . . a condition." For Miller it was a condition and not a "theory that confronts [the African American]."[44]

For Du Bois, the concept of an African American class structure grew out of his attempt to rebut Hoffman's prediction of the impending extinction of African Americans. To Du Bois, writing in the *Annals of the American Academy of Political and Social Sciences* in 1897, it was apparent that Hoffman did not have the insight to offer a "proper interpretation of apparently contradictory social facts . . . if for instance, we find among American Negroes today, at the very same time, increasing intelligence and increasing crime, increasing wealth and disproportionate poverty, increasing religious and moral activity and high rate of illegitimacy in births, we can no more fasten upon the bad as typifying the general tendency than we can upon the good."[45]

Arguing emphatically against Hoffman's assertion that the negative tendencies pertained to "the race" rather than to the class structure that had developed since emancipation, Du Bois believed that the extent of the African American's progress or retrogression was determined by the individual's rank within the black social structure.[46] He was certain that white prejudice was an obstacle to black progress because it kept more blacks in the lower class.

Like Miller and Du Bois, Work took to task Hoffman's argument that African Americans had not improved their own moral and social lives. Furthermore, like his fellow African American social scientists, he thought the retrogression-progression binary was far more complex than Hoffman assumed, insofar as Hoffman viewed the so-called racial traits as the sole cause of their alleged retrogression. Like Du Bois, Work stressed the significance of socioeconomic factors in any discussion of morality of whites vis-à-vis blacks.

Work based his long article on an enormous amount of descriptive statistical data on crime perpetrated by African Americans in Chicago. Work sought to determine whether crime was "increasing or decreasing, and how this crime compares with other peoples of the city, and the country in general." In reference to the first query, Work found that in Chicago since 1872, there had been "a very large increase in the number of negro arrests in proportion to the whole number of arrests."[47] In reference to the second query, he found that "the ratio of negro arrests to the negro population" was nearly six times as great as the proportion of arrests in the total population in 1896. In reference to the third query, in which he compared African American arrests in Chicago to those in New York City, Washington, D.C., Richmond, Virginia, and Charleston, South Carolina, Chicago's ratio was highest. Yet, despite Work's admission that African American crime was increasing in Chicago, the article contained a subtext in which he sought to explain the high crime rate. Work pointed out that most of the crimes took place in the slums of the city, which had high rates of unemployment and which contained few churches and missions and no settlement houses. Furthermore, most crimes were committed by young, unemployed, single men and women. Most of the perpetrators of crime by African Americans in Chicago, in short, were the underclass of the late 1890s. Work concluded that crimes committed by African Americans were due to the fact that "he [the African American] is in this transitional state from a lower to a higher plane of development." Although Work conceded to Darwinians that some of the criminality was a result of "race characteristics peculiar to [the African American]," he nevertheless went on to declare that "the economic phase of this transition . . . accounts for a large part of the excess of negro crime in the United States."[48]

Although Work did not specify the nature of African Americans' "race characteristics" or their source, it is clear that he was attempting to situate his position between racial determinism and economic determinism—an ambiguous position that on the one hand could unwittingly excuse the harsh and brutal conditions to which most African Americans were subjected and on the other could indict those conditions by pointing to the vast majority of African Americans' economic positions. Despite his entanglement in the labyrinth of the progressive evolutionist argument, Work was nevertheless definitely not a subscriber to white supremacy, which posited the permanent inferiority of African Americans, for he felt that his race—through the Lamarckian inheritance of acquired characteristics—possessed the capacity to evolve to a higher plane in the social order.

Work received his Ph.B. in sociology in 1902 and completed his master's thesis in 1903 in the same discipline. In his thesis, "The Negro Real Estate Owners of Chicago," he argued that African Americans were making progress, insofar as the number of African American real estate owners as well as the value of their holdings were increasing. Work's thesis is one of the most important contributions to the study of the enterprise of Chicago's African Americans during this period. Work's penchant for William I. Thomas's emphasis on historical particularism and his own environmental approach to the differences of whites and blacks ran counter to widely held and sincerely felt hereditarian and racial discourses.

Work documented the history of blacks in Illinois in general and Chicago in particular from the eighteenth century to the beginning of the twentieth century. He carefully documented the act adopted by the territorial legislature in Illinois in 1812 that permitted slaveholders to bring "slaves over fifteen years of age into the territory, and having indentured and registered them, to continue them in servitude under certain conditions," the abolition of "indentured slavery" in 1848; the Black Laws that rendered the free blacks into a pariah class; and the free blacks' formal protest against the Black Laws, which were repealed in 1866.[49] Work noted, however, the variability of race relations in Illinois. In Chicago, for example, he stated that African Americans "did not have as much prejudice to contend with . . . as in other parts of the state. They were more secure in their rights and privileges." Chicago's exceptionalism in Illinois history stemmed from such historical factors as its position as "one of the most important stations of the underground railway" and the opportunities it offered "industrious workers."[50]

Furthermore, Work pointed out that during the period between the founding of Chicago by the San Domingan Jean Baptiste DuSable in 1780 to the Chicago fire of 1874, the data on property owning by African Americans were "not sufficient to warrant any statement." After the fire of 1874, in which "Negro property was almost wiped out," Negro property owning in Chicago increased proportionately with the rapid increase in population. A consequence, Work noted, was "the recent rise of Negro Real Estate dealers, nine of whom are found in the city, and through whom most of the present buying is done. A considerable amount of the renting is also through their agency."[51] Work saved his parting shots for the system of de facto residential segregation. He wrote:

> The work of segregation is applied especially to the Negroes so that almost all of them are compelled to live in segregated and undesirable districts. The methods used to insure segregation [are] to charge Negroes a higher rent than is charged other people, for property outside of the Black Belt, or to refuse to sell property except in particular neighborhoods, and to refuse to sell property except in particular localities. The effect of this is to mass the best and worst classes of the Negroes together.[52]

As a consequence, most blacks lived in overcrowded, unsanitary districts, paid high rents, and were lumped together with the "lewd and vicious" elements of the black population. For work, the solution lay in some self-help measures—that is, "a larger investment on the part of the Negroes themselves in homes outside of congested localities; an enlargement of the districts in which they may live, and more and better property as regards sanitations, etc. which they may rent at moderate prices."[53] Like Du Bois and most members of the African American elite who were proponents of the uplift ideology, Work thought most lower-class persons were more prone to immoral activities; as a consequence, he thought they should be kept at a distance until such time that they were elevated.

Work obtained a job at Georgia State Industrial College in Savannah—an institution of which the father of Richard R. Wright Jr. was president. Receiving his master of arts in divinity from the Department of Sociology at the University of Chicago in 1903, Work marked the first awarding of an advanced degree to an African American by that institution. For Work, his achievement was not an indication of any special innate mental ability that he possessed. Instead it indicated to him determination and perseverance—essential character traits that Work thought would enable any person in the United States to succeed. In fact, he would later remark, in reference to his successful quest for his degrees at the University of Chicago: "There were, of course, many hardships and trials, but no more, perhaps less, than would come to anyone who had to educate himself through his own exertions. My motto is do all that you can, do not let the fact that you . . . have a much greater handicap deter you. For all things are possible to him that is willing to make the sacrifice."[54]

Although we can only speculate why Work chose to go south, we do know that he had already begun a collaboration with W. E. B. Du Bois, which was to last approximately five years. Du Bois, who had begun the tasks not only of amassing a large body of empirical data on African Americans in order to counter the propaganda of extreme racists but also to prod African Americans out of their inertia and thereby to induce them to participate in voluntaristic institutions, attracted both Work and Richard R. Wright Jr. to research and write *The Negro Church* in 1903. Work would spend the rest of his career in the South. During these years, he published three articles in Du Bois's *Atlanta University Publications:* "The Middle West, Illinois" (1903); "Crime in Cities" (1904); and "The Negro Brain" (1906). Furthermore, Work collaborated with Du Bois and Wright in a study of sharecropping in Lownde's County, Alabama, in 1906.

The first piece, which was coauthored with Du Bois, traced the evolution of the Negro church in the Midwest in general and Illinois in particular, from the postbellum period to his day. Work and Du Bois argued that conditions in freedom had "modified" the church's emphasis on the "emotional side of mentality and the future life"—primarily in the Baptist and Methodist churches. In Chicago, in particular, "there are some churches where the emphasis is placed sometimes on the emotional, the future life, sometimes on the intellectual and this present life," Du Bois and Work observed. "There is a large number of churches in which the emphasis is almost entirely on the intellectual and the things of this life," they noted with approval. Thus, both sociologists of African American ancestry concluded: "It may be said, therefore, that in general the farther the people have moved from slavery conditions the less emotional and unpractical they are religiously; the more effort there is to make religion a rule of conduct for everyday life."[55] At that time, Work, in essence, was espousing liberal Christianity—a great difference from the Ethiopianism he would later adopt.

Work's experiences in Chicago reinforced (and sometimes challenged) his conservative worldview. The preachings and activism of prominent social gospel ministers challenged his traditional worldview. Furthermore, he had been influenced by the "scientific sociology" of William I. Thomas. As a consequence, beneath the layers of descriptive statistics that would characterize the articles he wrote while living in Chicago, Work would conclude that the destructive impact of northern, urban living conditions—not the presumed "racial traits" that Frederick L. Hoffman assumed obtained—made the communal existence of many African Americans burdensome. Work, nevertheless, truly believed that a degree of initiative and perseverance in the forms of institutional development, voluntarism, and education could succeed in repairing the damage. In short, during this period Work never wavered from his commitment to socioeconomic advancement through education and property ownership.

The Second Period, 1903–8

At the beginning of the twentieth century, the African American intelligentsia was well aware that the issues of African Americans' status and rights in the foreseeable future were inextricably bound to two initiatives—the development of effective strategies, first, to dismantle the twin incubus of disfranchisement and Jim Crow and, second, to uplift the African American masses to the point where they could enjoy the freedom and prosperity of first-class citizenship. Though they were far from an agreement on the tactics to be employed on the first initiative (as was evident in the great debate between Booker T. Washington and W. E. B. Du Bois), there was substantial agreement on the premium value of the education of whites and blacks in social sciences. The search for "scientific" truth in those disciplines would result in the accumulation of knowledge that would eventually undermine the bases of the justification for the differential treatment of blacks.

The second phase of Work's career in research lasted from 1903 to 1908. Work had perhaps become familiar with the research of the nation's leading anthropologist, Franz "Uri" Boas, while studying under William I. Thomas at the University of Chicago. During his collaboration with Du Bois in the Atlanta studies, Work drew on the publications of Boas. Boas was a German-born, Jewish immigrant who had come to the United States in 1887, where he encountered virulent anti-Semitism. Despite his difficulties in securing and holding employment, Boas's brilliant work resulted in his appointment as professor of anthropology at Columbia University, where he remained until his death in 1942.

Franz Boas was born in 1858 in Minden, Westphalia, Germany, into a freethinking Jewish household. Upon reaching maturity, he attended several German universities, Heidelberg, Bonn, and Kiel, receiving his doctorate in physics in Kiel in 1881. After a year in the German army and another two years of studying, Boas went to Baffinland on an expedition to do the cultural geography of the Eskimos. His experiences among the Eskimos, however, sowed the seeds of his attempt to understand the laws of human nature and, as a consequence, to make the gradual transition from cultural geography and ethnology to anthropology.

A turning point in Boas's life came in 1887, when he emigrated to the United States, hoping for career opportunities that were absent in the conservative, anti-Semitic workplace of Bismarck's Germany. Yet for almost a decade after his arrival in the United States, Boas confronted tremendous obstacles in securing and holding professional positions—primarily because of the virulent anti-Semitism that pervaded the nation.

Boas's employment crisis ended in 1896, when Frederic W. Putnam appointed him assistant curator at the American Museum of Natural History in New York City. He advanced to curator in 1901 while serving as a lecturer at Columbia University in 1899, a position he held until his death in 1942. Before 1920, Boas had trained such prominent anthropologists as Alfred L. Kroeber, Robert H. Lowie, Edward Sapir, and Alexander A. Goldenweiser. Students trained after 1920 included Melville J. Herskovits, Ruth Benedict, Margaret Mead, Ashley Montagu, and Otto Klineberg. Furthermore, Boas influenced perceptibly the thought of Booker T. Washington, W. E. B. Du Bois, Carter G. Woodson, Alain L. Locke, George E. Haynes, Abram Harris, Charles S. Johnson, Charles H. Thompson, and Zora Neale Hurston—African American intellectuals who were in the forefront of the antiracist thinkers. Boas's impact on the composition of anthropology in the United States was so great that in the 1950s, virtually all of the anthropologists in the country had studied under Boas or one of his students. Boas's scholarship—especially his path-breaking work *The Mind of Primi-*

tive Man (1911)—profoundly influenced the concepts of "race" and "culture," not only in his times but also in our own. Debunking the concept of "race" as a supraindividual organic entity and the concept of cultural hierarchies, Boas is almost single-handedly responsible for ushering in modern conceptions of race and cultural relativism.

Boas responded to the dominant racist discourse in anthropology in three ways. First, he utilized the tools of anthropometry to generate new facts on which antiracist claims could be based. Second, he used scientific reasoning to question racist explanations of the facts. Third, he drew on both physical and cultural anthropology to remove markers by relabeling supposedly "peculiar" racial traits as universal human traits. Boas demonstrated that there was an *approximate* equality of whites and blacks by showing that the sizes of the cranial cavities of the two so-called races overlapped, and by highlighting evidence of the historical and present achievements of the peoples of Western and Central Africa, he strengthened Work's belief that people of African descent possessed the innate capabilities to progress.

During these years, Work published an article in the Atlanta University series entitled "The Negro Brain," which applied Boas's arguments on the sizes of the cranial cavities of whites and blacks to the brain weights of the two groups. "In connection with the well established fact that those characters which are said to be distinctive of particular races are found with more or less frequency in other races," Work argued, his findings "seem to indicate that what has been described as being peculiar in the size, shape and anatomy of the Negro brain is not true of all Negro brains." He concluded in a cogent fashion that "these peculiarities can no doubt be found in many white brains and probably have no special connection with the mental capacity of either race."[56]

Work, who was also evincing an interest in Africa, wrote a series of articles for the *Southern Workman.* The articles Work published in that organ reflected his extensive research in the major contemporary works on African life.[57]

For Work, Africans were people who had made, and were perfectly capable of making, in the present and future, achievements essential to human progress. Work, in short, as this point in his life, told rational scientific myths—based on the best information on Africans during his times—that reinforced one another and formed the historical element in the attempt to discredit the status quo. In a few years, he would completely alter the way Booker T. Washington conceived of African Americans' despised ancestors. Between 1899 and 1908, Washington had conceived of his African ancestors as primitive barbarians. In so doing, Work would reinforce Washington's belief in the ability of African Americans to progress, thereby further distancing Washington's position from that of the partisan purveyors of white supremacy.

In 1908, Thomas Jesse Jones, who taught sociology at Hampton Institute, was appalled by the factual errors in Booker T. Washington's speeches. Jones urged Washington to contact Work and characterized Work as "the man to get his facts for him." As a result, Washington contacted Work, who in 1908 recalled the story about Washington's recruitment effort as follows:

> Mr. Washington wrote to me and said he wanted to establish a department of history at Tuskegee in which there would be an opportunity for the study of the Negro. He had been urged to have a study made of graduates of Tuskegee. He wrote to me that he wanted to see me and said he was coming through Savannah. He was in his private car going to Beaufort, South Carolina to make a speech. I met him and said to him, "I have your letter." He said, "Yes, come over to Tuskegee and we'll talk it over." The conversation was just a minute and didn't consume as much time as it takes to tell you about it.[58]

However, in his "Autobiographical Sketch," written in 1940, Work portrayed himself as taking a more assertive role in the negotiations with Washington. When the latter asked him "to establish a department of Negro history," Work indicated that in his "opinion it would be more important and valuable to have a department specializing in the compiling of current data relating to the Negro. My suggestion was accepted and at Tuskegee Institute was established the first department, in a Negro Educational Institution, devoted to compiling from all available sources data relating to every phase of Negro life and history."[59]

Linda O. McMurry has suggested that the primary reason Work deserted Du Bois in 1908 for a position as director of the Tuskegee Institute Department of Records and Research was because of his disillusionment with Du Bois's transition from scholar to propagandist; yet, perhaps there were other factors that impinged on his decision to join Booker T. Washington. In an article entitled "Booker T. Washington, Pioneer," published in the "Inter-Racial Cooperation" department of the *Journal of Social Forces,* published by the southern white liberal Howard W. Odum in 1925, Work revealed why he admired the Tuskegee Wizard:

> Booker T. Washington's preaching concerning the dignity of labor, making education common, becoming efficient, he put into practice by developing at Tuskegee Institute a system of education which dignified labor, made education common and increased economic efficiency of the Negro. The development of Tuskegee Institute met the objectives of the Negroes with regard to

> labor in that they saw it in a new light. This development met the objectives of the North in that the people there saw that the Negro was being trained to take his place as a man and a citizen. It helped to remove the opposition in the South to Negro education, for by connecting education with every day life, it was made practical and a benefit not only to the Negro but also the South.[60]

In the ambience of Tuskegee Institute, Work was fortunate to reinforce Washington's conviction that blacks possessed the capacity to become self-reliant and progress by demonstrating the empowering attributes of an accurate portrayal of Africans, and by collecting statistical data on many aspects of African American life, including the effects of Alabama's temperance laws, crime rates among blacks, lynching, the rates of black participation in county and state fairs, the rates of the movement of blacks to the cities in the South, the comparative rates of blacks and whites operating farms, and the amount of money blacks contributed to the support of colleges, normal schools, and public schools.[61]

The preponderance of evidence in the Washington-Work correspondence indicates that the Tuskegee Wizard not only dictated to his subordinate the research questions to be addressed but also suggested the answers he wanted. For example, in 1910, Washington wrote to Work in reference to an article he wanted written on the progress of African Americans in Durham, North Carolina; Washington's "idea" was "to have you [Work] get data including figures, etc., as well as general information showing the progress that the colored people are making in the tobacco factories, in all lines of business, and, of course, bringing in the progress they are making in school and church work, but the business and industrial sides I want emphasized most." Washington concluded by urging Work "to plan your memorandum upon the work of the local Business League of Durham, that is the only way I can make a connection between Tuskegee and Durham, and the only justification I can find for having you go to Durham and do this work. You might begin with the statement, if you can justify it, that a large part of this progress in Durham grows out of the work of the Local Negro Business League."[62]

Clearly, Washington saw Work's role as gatherer of data for his propaganda machine. Acknowledging his services to the machine, on another occasion Washington wrote to Work thanking him "most heartily for preparing these figures for me [Washington] and to let you know how very valuable I consider them. It is impossible to go on placing these great truths before our race without great good being accomplished."[63]

Despite Jim Crow laws, disfranchisement, lynching, and economic oppression, Work showed that blacks were progressing. Unfortunately, Washington had been influenced by nineteenth-century racist conceptions of Africans throughout his childhood and most of his adult life. Initially, he considered his African ancestors to have been primitive barbarians. Work did much to modify his position and to convince him that Africans had made significant contributions to world civilization.

As early as the winter of 1903–4, Washington had begun writing a two-volume history of the Negro in Africa and America for Doubleday, Page and Company. In 1906, he assigned the writing of the work to Robert Ezra Park. Yet when work of higher priority flooded Park's desk, it was put aside. Two years later, after the insistence of the publisher, the writing of the volumes was assigned to Alvis Octavious Stafford, a teacher at the Institute for Colored Youth in Cheyney, Pennsylvania. The drafts that Stafford sent back were so poor that Work, the new director of Records and Research, and Park were called in to salvage the project.[64]

Park, who would go on to become the leading student of race relations after 1915, wrote to Washington concerning Work's contribution to the project:

> I think I ought, now as "The Story of the Negro" is off our hands, to say something of the way in which Mr. Work has helped me during this long, tedious, and often very discouraging task. From the very first, although the work I was doing was not anything he felt responsible for and although the demands I made upon him often interfered with his own work, he has never shirked or complained. He has met every demand I made upon him in perfect cheerfulness, and has done the work I asked him to do, as faithfully as if he were working at some task of his own choosing, and according to his own methods and ideas.[65]

In a series of articles that had appeared in the *Southern Workman* between 1906 and 1909 and *The Story of the Negro,* Work had quoted the most heralded authority, Boas, on the art of smelting ores by Africans, the artistic industries of Africa, the agriculture of Africans, native African culture, African law, and the character of African states.[66]

In the year following Washington's death, Work revealed why he thought that the knowledge that he had been acquiring since his graduate school days on Africa and Africans was of paramount importance in the evolution of an African American identity. Indeed, he was optimistic about the creation of this new identity. Work noted that anthropologists no longer treated "the true Negro race as peoples whose physical characteristics indicated their inferiority." No longer would the descriptions that "caricaturists seized upon . . . and popularized . . . in cartoons, in songs and in other ways," compel the African American "to believe in his inherent inferiority and that to attain superiority he must become like the white man in color, in achievements and, in fact, along all lines."[67] Work then linked the egalitarian ethnic pluralism of social gospel proponents such as Reverdy Ransom to Du Bois's notion of racial distinctiveness. He asked the following question: "Why cannot the Negro attain superiority along lines of his own, that is, instead of simply patterning after what the white man has done, why cannot the Negro through music, art, history, and science, make his own special contributions to the progress of the world?"[68]

For Work, the negation of the white supremacist argument that innate characteristics prevented blacks from excelling in "high" culture rested on Boas's empirical data. Work turned to the findings of Boasian anthropology as the basis for the claim that "while there are differences of races, there are no characteristics which *per se* indicate that one race is inferior or superior to another." This said, Work did not invoke the color-blind universalistic doctrine. He followed Boas's lead and suggested that there were racial hereditary aptitudes. "The existing differences" (though he did not specify what those differences were), he argued, "are differences in kind not in value." Yet Work also wanted to argue for the potency of the environment in the attainment of racial achievements and concluded that "whatever superiority one race has attained over another has largely been due to environment."[69] In this article, Work, however, did not provide any details in his discussion in reference to the nature-versus-nurture debate.

Although Work, like Boas, was caught between beliefs in "racial" differences and environmentalism, it must be remembered that he viewed his task as enhancing African Americans' self-esteem. In so doing, Work believed that he could aid the task of African American uplift that Washington had set as his goal. After surveying the achievements of Africans in the years before European colonization, Work wrote:

> From this brief sketch which I have given of the African in ancient and medieval times it is clear that Negroes should not despise the rock from which they were hewn. As a race they have a past which is full of interest. It is worthy of serious study. From it we can draw inspiration; for it appears that not all black men everywhere throughout the ages have been "hewers of wood and drawers of water." On the contrary, through long periods of time there were powerful black nations which have left the records of achievements and of which we are just now beginning to learn a little. This little, however, which we have learned teaches us that the Negroes of today should work and strive. Along their own special line and in their own peculiar way they should endeavor to make contributions to civilization.[70]

Work concluded the article in a manner reminiscent of the Ethiopianism of Alexander Crummell—the first African American to graduate from Cambridge University, erstwhile missionary to Liberia, and Episcopalian minister—and Du Bois. Crummell was an idealist and was critical of Washington's crass, materialistic philosophy. Nonetheless, it is necessary, as one of Crummell's biographers, J. R. Oldfield, has correctly pointed out, "not to exaggerate the differences in" Washington's and Crummell's positions. "Both men thought that blacks could not leap to greatness or superiority, both men believed that blacks had a special contribution to make to American society, and both men were concerned to instill in blacks a high moral and religious tone," Oldfield writes.[71] It should also be added that both shared the belief in Ethiopianism, which Work adopted. Reflecting Crummell's pride in "Ethiopia's black race," Work was certain that the achievements of African Americans could be of such magnitude that "once more black will be dignified and the fame of Ethiopia again spread throughout the world."[72] In this article, Work had clearly moved from telling rational, scientific myths—that is, narratives of Africa and Africans based on the works of the most competent authorities on those subjects—to mysticism—the narratives based on African American folk mythologies.

After 1908, white supremacists could take little comfort in Washington's philosophy. The contribution of Monroe N. Work to the evolution of Washington's thought was a reconfiguring of Washington's image of Africa and Africans, which caused all the myths employed before 1908 to collapse.

The Final Period

In the final stages of his career, Work clearly embraced a purely empirical worldview in which he sought to document empirically both the achievements of African Americans and to indict Anglo-Americans in the South for their past and contemporaneous crimes against humanity. Nevertheless, to the end, he was an optimist who believed that economic forces would revolutionize race relations in the region. His task, as he conceived of it, was to counter the irrational forces of racism and reaction that pervaded the South.

During the years after Washington's death, Work published several papers that included data indicating that African Americans had made tremendous economic, educational, health, and political progress since emancipation.[73] In particular, in one article, which was published in the *Publications of the American Sociological Society* in 1924, Work pointed out, as Robert E. Park would also do four years later, that African American progress exacerbated racial tensions between whites and blacks in urban-industrial areas. "The agitation and friction," he argued cogently, "now going on as to where Negroes shall live in cities centers about the efforts of progressive intelligent members of the groups to secure better places to live."[74] Work's emphasis on the progress that some African Americans had made was a theme that many prominent sociologists such as Robert Ezra Park, Howard W. Odum, and Thomas J. Woofter would adopt in the 1930s and 1940s.[75]

For Work, the key to intraracial self-reliance and progress lay in exposing African Americans to the facts. In 1924, he wrote: "The lines along which we should have race knowledge are three; namely, those relating to racial characteristics; those relating to our past history and those relating to the present conditions and status of the group."[76] Work believed that collecting facts along those lines was significant, for "no sort of propaganda is, in the end, so effective as the facts themselves."[77] Thus, in the latter years of his life, when it was apparent that African American farmers were being removed from their land, Work turned to the issues of race and class with a knowledge of the facts that few persons could muster. Insofar as land tenure in the South was concerned, he argued cogently, "both racial factors and economic factors were operating." "The racial factors are endeavoring to maintain differences based on race," Work stated, "while at the same time, economic forces which are more or less impersonal, are operating to place on the same level all of the individuals in a particular class regardless of race."[78] In the end, Work predicted erroneously that the problems confronting blacks and whites would be resolved. He stated: "As the new economy, agricultural-industrial economy, comes more and more into the South, there will be greater and greater conformity between the economic order and the political and moral order. . . . The new economy will provide a situation in which there will be not only economic cooperation between race and race, and between class and class, so that the interests of all the people will be concerned."[79]

Furthermore, Work's *Negro Year Book* and *Annual Encyclopedia,* nine volumes of which he edited between 1912 and 1938, were reviewed favorably in such prestigious scholarly journals as the *Journal of Negro History,* the *Journal of Applied Sociology,* the *American Journal of Sociology, Social Service Review,* the *American Sociological Review,* and *Rural Sociology.* In 1936, E. Franklin Frazier, noted author and the head of the Department of Sociology at Howard University, stated unequivocally that it would be difficult to supersede "in scholarly character or usefulness . . . the present *Negro Year Book* the limitations of which may be excused on the grounds that it represents the pioneer efforts of a single person who has been forced to work with inadequate resources."[80] In addition, Work's book *A Bibliography of the Negro in Africa and America,* which was published by the H. W. Wilson Company in 1928, was a bibliographic masterpiece. The volume, which was favorably reviewed in the *Crisis,* the *Journal of Negro History, Sociology and Social Research,* and the *Annals of the American Academy of Political and Social Science,* was a monumental contribution to scholarship and expressed his valiant attempt to inspire the confidence of African Americans. Furthermore, Work was also an activist. Washington had founded the Tuskegee Negro Conference to remedy the problems of African American farmers, fought surreptitiously against disfranchisement and Jim Crow, sponsored legal action against peonage, supported the prohibition movement, and founded the National Negro Business League to assist African American businessmen. Like his mentor, Work established a National Negro Health Week and published the *Tuskegee Lynching Report,* which contained descriptive statistics that were distributed to hundreds of newspapers. In addition, he actively sought to increase the number of black registered voters in Macon County, Alabama.

To sum up, although Work participated in the Niagara Movement, he eschewed, for the most part, the early campaign for civil and political rights. In the end, like Booker T. Washington, Work was a racial moderate. Furthermore, although he vacillated between scientism and mysticism and between a Christian universalism and Ethiopianism, it is clear that, as best as he was allowed by the caste system, he took gradual steps—collecting data that contradicted those who argued that African Americans were retrogressing and in the future there would be no place for them in society, and creating viable myths in reference to Africa—to demonstrate that Washington's program of self-help was a realistic alternative to surrendering to the forces that conspired to renounce the humanity of African Americans. Indeed, Work was a forebear of the civil rights movement.

Conclusion

For scholars who examine and analyze the germination, maturation, demise, and revival of particular ideas from one historical epoch to another, the malleability of most ideas is axiomatic. Yet the questions of how and why certain ideas retain their essential valuations for centuries are, for most historians of ideas, more problematic—especially in the case of an idea as volatile as that of race.[1]

The persistence of the idea of race perhaps stems from the fact that the beliefs and values of peoples play as significant a role as the modes of production in material life in determining the course of history, for the way events are interpreted is often a result of the particular religious or social beliefs held sacred by a people. Most people react in terms of what they perceive to be true, and often no amount of discreditation—however "artful" or "scientific"—of their myths can change them.[2]

The aforementioned observations are implicit in the statement by one of the leading historians of race, George M. Fredrickson, in his collection of essays in *The Arrogance of Race* (1988)—that most people hold with passionate fallacies that are "not destined to collapse because they are in conflict with empirical reality."[3] For Fredrickson, the persistence of racial essentialist theory stems, in short, from a people's delusions. The leading historian of African American nationalism, Wilson J. Moses, has concurred with Fredrickson's observations. In reference to African American popular history, Moses argued, in his controversial collection of essays *Afrotopia* (1998), that as long as there is a separate black population, the particularistic, "historical myths and values" of African Americans are bound to be with us. To be more precise, Moses argues, they will be with us for the "foreseeable future."[4] In other words, Moses believes the persistence of racial essentialist history stems not only from a people's delusions, as Fredrickson has suggested, but also from its particularistic history.

Nevertheless, I will argue that racial essentialist narratives penned by African Americans in response to European Americans' prejudiced narratives of the classical era are reactive responses that should be avoided by professional historians at all costs. An ideal vision of African American history, in other words, *should not* be based upon the type of mysticism that highlights some distant pharaohs and the achievements of peoples who were only remotely connected with the peoples of medieval West and Central Africa. Egyptocentrism—which Wilson J. Moses differentiates from "Afrocentrism"—at the turn of the twentieth century served a corrective function, insofar as it discredited, as W. E. B. Du Bois pointed out astutely, the white racial essentialists' "assumptions . . . that color is a mark of inferiority."[5] Nevertheless, it must be emphasized, as the historian Maghan Keita has asserted in reference to present-day claims of Egyptocentrists, that these arguments clash with those of the distinguished classicist Frank M. Snowden. Although Keita admits that Snowden embraced "Ethiopianism," he observes that "Snowden is correct in insisting that the classical era knew none of the racial categorization of the modern world, nor its implication."[6]

Fortunately, since the 1980s, both African American and European American scholars have focused on the lives, thoughts, and actions of leading African American figures, both male and female, who came of age during the Gilded Age and the Progressive Era—the period usually designated the "nadir" by scholars of African American history, such as Rayford W. Logan.[7] These historians have avoided the pitfalls of uncritical, racial essentialist narratives. Although they have celebrated the triumphs of individuals who succeeded in accomplishing much, despite the odds and the obdurateness of racism, these scholars do not underestimate the extent to which individuals such as W. E. B. Du Bois, Archibald Grimké, John Hope, Lugenia Burns Hope, Carter G. Woodson, Booker T. Washington, William Hannibal Thomas, and Ida Barnett-Wells were scarred and embittered in the course of reaching the heights they achieved. Furthermore, although historians of the African American experience of this period celebrate the agency of leading personages, they nevertheless do not ignore the extent to which the gifted individuals' options were limited and circumscribed by the predominance of European American ethnocentrism and racism.[8] Suffice it to say that these historians show a universalism with a particularistic bent—insofar as they analyze and depict the failures as well as the triumphs of individuals of African American descent who were able to overcome the hardships of desperation, isolation, and self-doubt that were attendant not only to their caste-like status but also to their humanity.

Despite the fact that these scholars have presented us with much important information in reference to the agency of African Americans and charted their accomplishments and contributions to the United States of America, they are perhaps mistaken in their notion that when European Americans learn these things, they will no longer embrace the prejudicial attitudes and exercise or tacitly accept discriminatory behavior by those among them, or that African Americans will feel less marginalized and thereby gain greater self-esteem because of their endeavors. Nevertheless, this information is very important—primarily because, as Du Bois noted in *The Negro,* "Whatever it is fair to predicate of the mass of human beings may be predicated of the Negro."[9]

We do know, however, that there are insidious motives behind the persistence of white, racial essentialism in both its naïve expressions and sophistical guises. The anthropologist Audrey Smedley has pointed out correctly, in reference to the idea of race, that "[It] continues in large part because of its value as a mechanism for identifying who should have access to wealth, privilege, loyalty, respect and power and who should not. . . . It [the idea of race] is a powerful psychological force, providing scapegoat functions as well as facile external means of establishing and measuring one's own self-worth." For Smedley, the idea of race was "a folk classification . . . a cosmological ordering system structured out of the political, economic, and social realities of peoples who had emerged as expansionist, conquering, dominating nations on a worldwide quest for wealth and power." This "folk classification" was incorporated into the scientific and legal discourses by the end of the eighteenth century in order for elites to rationalize and justify the existing northern and western European dominance over Native Americans and persons of discernible African ancestry.[10] As a consequence, by the end of the nineteenth century, the hereditarian perspective sought to prove that there were biological differences in the intelligence and the behavior of the so-called races.

The aforementioned observations notwithstanding, some sociologists, such as James B. McKee and Chris Smaje, contend that it is not necessary to deconstruct "racial essentialism," primarily "because"—to use Smaje's words—"naïve essentialism no longer has any intellectual credibility."[11] Smaje himself, however, seems unfamiliar with the racial politics of American university personnel and life in the United States of America—or is not able or willing to recognize racism's naïve and sophistical guises. Put another way, during the past decade, the reopening of the issue of differential scores between whites and blacks on IQ tests—and I do unequivocally argue that the assertion of the purported lower intelligence of a disproportional number of persons of African American descent vis-à-vis European Americans can be naïve and/or sophistical racial essentialism—and hence the issue of African American intelligence in the United States have certainly raised the cachet of reargued racial essentialists in North American universities and think tanks. Furthermore, Smaje, who believes that universities are "natural" or "apolitical" entities and that sociological theories alone are incapable of solving political problems, has taken a position, despite his denial, that falls under the rubrics of fatalism, disinterestedness, and quietism.[12] Nevertheless, although racial essentialism is at present alive in some scholarly circles in the United States, its most blatant thrusts have been effectively contradicted by the vast majority of competent social scientists' research. As a consequence, a case can be made for the potency of activist scholarship within the academy, which has distinguished sociology from its origins to the present.

The award-winning, historically minded sociologist James B. McKee, who in *Sociology and the Race Problem* (1993), like Smaje, had espoused his longing for the return to a type of "disinterestedness" proposed by Robert E. Park and others, argued that most sociologists had abandoned racial essentialism by the 1930s, substituting in its place a cultural essentialism that stated that African Americans "were a culturally inferior people, not yet fit to participate in modern society," and furthermore "possessed no inherited culture of their own."[13] Professor McKee's thesis is simpleminded when compared to the influential scholarly work of W. Lloyd Warner and his associates and Hortense Powdermaker on the variability of caste, class, and culture in the United States.[14] McKee is obviously trying to strike a telling blow at proponents of the psychocultural deficit theory of African American deficiencies held by such scholars as Daniel P. Moynihan and Nathan Glazer. Proponents of this position argue that the psychocultural damage inflicted on African Americans by three hundred years of slavery and racial oppression has persisted to this day, and as a consequence, has affected adversely their initiative, character, conduct, and work habits. Present-day proponents' works—articulated most forcibly in the 1990s by D'inesh D'Souza—have shifted the argument of African American inferiority from the domains of race and class to the domain of cultures. In so doing, they assumed the cultural determinist stance and thereby avoided accusations of racism. Furthermore, they have also, with good reason, rejected the relativism of Franz "Uri" Boas and his disciples; for the United States has, in the recent past, been the ascendant economic power in the world, despite its racially segmented labor force.

However, social scientists such as W. Lloyd Warner, Allison Davis, Burleigh B. Gardner, Mary R. Gardner, Buford H. Junker, and Walter A. Adams recognized as early as the 1930s that caste (or racial) and cultural essentialism did not take into account interracial, as well as intraracial, class cultural differences. In other words, as I have argued elsewhere, sociology was never as univocal on the issue of racial and cultural essentialism as Professor McKee presumes; for Marxist-influenced scholars who have followed the lead of the late sociologist Oliver C. Cox have embraced implicitly egalitarian essentialist views. These sociologists suggest—and to my mind, they are correct on this issue—that the idea of race is a historical by-product of social relationships between people, which, too, is historical myth.[15]

In contradistinction to both history proper and sociology, anthropology, which has for almost a century been the most progressive social science discipline on the idea of race, has not exhibited the degree of continuity in its interrogation of that idea from the eighteenth to the twentieth centuries in North America that some present-day scholars might presume. As a consequence, the purpose of this book has been to adumbrate the history of anthropology from the late eighteenth to the late twentieth centuries. Hopefully, it will demonstrate the extent to which anthropology proper has reacted to major cultural reorientation in America. It also gives credence to Lee D. Baker's graphic wording that Boasian anthropology advances "research that exposes the contradictions in the U. S. society in an effort to reconcile the ideal of racial equality with the nagging, persistent, and seemingly perpetual forms of oppression."[16] Indeed, Boasian anthropology has called into question the validity of a bogus concept that seems to persist in public and private discourses, despite the protestations of many leading scholars to the contrary.

The historians Mia Bay, Sander L. Gilman, Nancy Leys Stepan, and Wilson J. Moses and historically minded anthropologists such as Lee D. Baker, Ira Harrison, Faye Harrison, and Carolyn Fluehr-Lobban have uncovered an oppositional yet fecund tradition of resistance on the part of black thinkers to the dominant "scientific" discourse on race in anthropology during the nineteenth and early twentieth centuries.[17] To my mind, however, an overemphasis on black agency—although the aforementioned scholars do fill out the narratives of anthropology's history—obscures the predominant extent to which most white practitioners of racial science were able to silence the opposition of black thinkers.

In closing, I would argue that, despite good intentions overall, the European American and African American antiracist traditions have been reactive rather than proactive. Since the parameters of the discourse on the purported relative abilities of the so-called races had been framed by nineteenth-century racists, Boas and his disciples found themselves working within a tradition from which they could not fully extricate themselves. As a result, Boas and his students' responses to "scientific racism" were compromised—a fact that helps account for our present-day discomfiture.

Notes

Introduction

1. Henry A. Bullock, *A History of Negro Education in the South, from 1619 to the Present* (Cambridge: Harvard University Press, 1968).

2. George W. Stocking Jr., *Race, Culture, and Evolution: Essays in the History of Anthropology* (New York: Free Press, 1968), 306.

3. Thomas F. Gossett, *Race: The History of an Idea in America* (Dallas: Southern Methodist University Press, 1963), 429.

4. I. A. Newby, *Jim Crow's Defense: Anti-Negro Thought in America, 1900–1930* (Baton Rouge: Louisiana State University Press, 1965), 197.

5. John P. Jackson Jr., *Social Scientists for Social Justice: Making the Case against Segregation* (New York: New York University Press, 2001), 7. For a recent clarification of his position, see John P. Jackson Jr., *Science for Segregation: Race, Law, and the Case against Brown v. Board of Education* (New York: New York University Press, 2005).

6. John L. Jackson Jr., *Harlem World: Doing Race and Class in Contemporary Black America* (Chicago: University of Chicago Press, 2001), 236 n. 17.

7. Regna Darnell, *Invisible Genealogies: A History of Americanist Anthropology* (Lincoln: University of Nebraska Press, 2001), 323.

Chapter 1: Historiographical Concerns in the History of Anthropology

Chapter 1 originally published as "Between Universalism and Particularism: Historiographical Concern in the History of Anthropology," *Journal of African American Studies* 7, no. 2 (2003): 61–68. © 2003 Transaction Publishers.

1. The historian of anthropology Hubert S. Lewis has pointed out that George W. Stocking Jr., in contradistinction to his professional historicism, fell "prey" to presentism in "Anthropology as *Kulterkamp:* Science and Politics in the Career of Franz Boas," in *The Enthnographer's Magic and Other Essays in the History of Anthropology* (Madison: University of Wisconsin Press, 1992), 110–13. See Hubert S. Lewis, "The Pas-

sion of Franz Boas," *American Anthropologist* 103 (June 2001): 462. See also Stocking's swipe at the present writer in his *Delimiting Anthropology: Occasional Inquiries and Reflections* (Madison: University of Wisconsin Press, 2001), 25–26.

2. George W. Stocking Jr., *Race, Culture, and Evolution: Essays in the History of Anthropology* (New York: Free Press, 1968); *The Ethnographer's Magic; After Tylor: British Social Anthropology* (Madison: University of Wisconsin Press, 1993).

3. Nancy L. Stepan, *The Idea of Race in Science: Great Britain, 1800–1960* (London: Macmillan, 1982), xv.

4. My dissertation, "The Afro-American in American Sociological Literature, 1895–1945," completed under the tutelage of a great historian of both evangelical Protestantism and the Cherokees, William G. McLoughlin; the sociologist Harold Pfautz, and historian of Africana studies Rhett S. Jones, in the American Civilization Program (now Department) at Brown University in 1977, was the foundation for this book.

5. Lewis, "The Passion of Franz Boas," 447.

6. Stocking, *The Ethnographer's Magic,* 8.

7. Ira E. Harrison and Faye V. Harrison, eds., *African American Pioneers in Anthropology* (Urbana: University of Illinois Press, 1999), 4.

8. Micaela di Leonardo, *Exotics at Home, Anthropologies, Others, American Modernity* (Chicago: University of Chicago Press, 1998), 21, 9.

9. St. Clair Drake, "Anthropology and the Black Experience," *Black Scholar* 11, no. 7 (1980): 6.

10. Wilson J. Moses, *Afrotopia: The Roots of African American Popular History* (Cambridge, England: Cambridge University Press, 1998); Stephen Howe, *Afrocentrism: Mythical Pasts and Imagined Homes* (London: Verso, 1998); Mia Bay, *The White Image in the Black Mind: African American Ideas about White People, 1830–1925* (New York: Oxford University Press, 2000); Maghan Keita, *Race and the Writing of History: Riddling the Sphinx* (New York: Oxford University Press, 2001); Clarence E. Walker, *We Can't Go Home Again: An Argument about Afrocentrism* (New York: Oxford University Press, 2001).

11. Quoted in Greg Thomas, "The Black Studies," *Village Voice,* January 17, 1995, 5.

12. Howe, *Afrocentrism,* 12.

13. Bay, *The White Image in the Black Mind,* 229.

14. Keita, *Race and the Writing of History,* introduction.

15. Walker, *We Can't Go Home,* xxiv.

16. Drake, "Anthropology and the Black Experience," 12–14.

17. Bay, *The White Image in the Black Mind;* Sander L. Gilman and Nancy L. Stepan, "Appropriating the Idioms of Science: The Rejection of Scientific Racism," in *The Bounds of Race: Perspectives on Hegemony and Resistance,* ed. Dominick La Capra (Ithaca, N.Y.: Cornell University Press, 1991), 72–103; Moses, *Afrotopia;* Lee D. Baker, *From Savage to Negro: Anthropology and the Construction of Race, 1896–1954* (Berkeley: University of California Press, 1998); Harrison and Harrison, *African American Pioneers in Anthropology;* and Carolyn Fluehr-Lobban, "Anténor Furmin: Haitian Pioneer of Anthropology," *American Anthropologist* (September 2000): 499–566.

18. Vernon J. Williams Jr., "Demythologizing the Myths of West Africa: George Washington Ellis and the Vai Peoples," *Griot* 14 (fall 1995): 42–47; Vernon J. Williams Jr., *Rethinking Race: Franz Boas and His Contemporaries* (Lexington: University Press of

Kentucky, 1996), 44–46, 78–84; Vernon J. Williams Jr., "A Gifted Amateur: The Case of George Washington Ellis," *American Anthropologist* 104 (June 2002): 544–50.

19. Williams, "A Gifted Amateur."

20. Ibid.

21. Ibid.

22. Ibid.

23. Ibid.

24. Baker, *From Savage to Negro;* Thomas C. Paterson, *A Social History of Anthropology in the United States* (Oxford: Berg, 2001), x.

Chapter 2: Franz Boas's Paradox and the African American Intelligentsia

Chapter 2 reprinted from *African Americans in the Twentieth Century: Studies in Convergence and Conflict,* ed. V. P. Franklin, Nancy L. Grant, Harold M. Kletnick, and Genna Rae McNeil, by permission of the University of Missouri Press. Copyright © 1998 by the Curators of the University of Missouri.

1. Marshall Hyatt, *Franz Boas—Social Activist: The Dynamics of Ethnicity* (New York: Greenwood Press, 1990), 4. See also Douglas Cole, *Franz Boas: The Early Years, 1858–1906* (Seattle: University of Washington Press, 1999).

2. Hyatt, *Franz Boas—Social Activist.*

3. George W. Stocking Jr., *Race, Culture, and Evolution: Essays in the History of Anthropology* (New York: Free Press, 1968), 143.

4. Quoted in Melville J. Herskovits, *Franz Boas: The Science of Man in the Making* (New York: Scribner's, 1953), 1.

5. Vernon J. Williams Jr., *From a Caste to a Minority: Changing Attitudes of American Sociologists toward Afro-Americans, 1896–1945* (Westport, Conn.: Greenwood Press, 1989), 34–57.

6. Stocking, *Race, Culture, and Evolution,* 189; George W. Stocking Jr., ed., *A Franz Boas Reader: The Shaping of American Anthropology, 1883–1911* (Chicago: University of Chicago Press, 1974), 220.

7. Franz Boas, "Human Faculty as Determined by Race," in Stocking, *A Franz Boas Reader,* 223–27.

8. Stocking, *Race, Culture and Evolution,* 163–64.

9. Quoted in Stephan Jay Gould, *The Mismeasure of Man* (New York: Norton, 1981), 87.

10. Boas, "Human Faculty as Determined by Race," 232.

11. William R. Stanton, *The Leopard's Spots: Scientific Attitudes toward Race in America, 1815–1859* (Chicago: University of Chicago Press, 1960).

12. Boas, "Human Faculty as Determined by Race," 316.

13. Quoted in John S. Haller Jr., *Outcasts from Evolution: Scientific Attitudes of Racial Inferiority, 1859–1900* (Urbana: University of Illinois Press, 1971), 178, 191; quoted in Gould, *The Mismeasure of Man,* 116.

14. Boas, "Human Faculty as Determined by Race," 230, 232.

15. William I. Thomas, "The Scope and Method of Folk-Psychology," *American Journal of Sociology* 1 (November 1895): 436–37.

16. Franz Boas, "The Mind of Primitive Man," *Journal of American Folk-Lore* 14 (January–March 1901): 1–11.

17. Boas, "Human Faculty as Determined by Race," 239.

18. Gilbert Osofsky, *Harlem: The Making of a Ghetto: Negro New York, 1890–1930* (New York: Harper and Row, 1963), chap. 2; Carole Marks, *Farewell—We're Good and Gone: The Great Black Migration* (Bloomington: Indiana University Press, 1989); James R. Grossman, *Land of Hope: Chicago, Black Southerners and the Great Migration* (Chicago: University of Chicago Press, 1989); George M. Fredrickson, *The Arrogance of Race: Historical Perspectives on Slavery, Racism, and Social Inequality* (Middletown, Conn.: Wesleyan University Press, 1988), 265.

19. Mary White Ovington, *Half a Man: The Status of the Negro in New York* (New York: Longmans, Green, 1915), ix; Franz Boas, "The Negro and the Demands of Modern Life," *Charities* 15 (October 1905): 86; and Franz Boas, "The Real Race Problem," *Crisis* 1 (December 1910): 22–25.

20. Boas, "The Negro and the Demands of Modern Life," 86.

21. Ibid., 87.

22. Franz Boas to Edward T. Devine, October 21, 1905, Franz Boas Papers, American Philosophical Society, Philadelphia (hereafter Boas Papers).

23. Franz Boas to Vladimir G. Simkhovich, March 15, 1906, Boas Papers.

24. Franz Boas to Felix Adler, October 10, 1906, Boas Papers.

25. Franz Boas to Reverend James Boddy, May 7, 1906, Boas Papers.

26. R. R. Wright Sr. to Franz Boas, January 2, 1907, and Franz Boas to R. R. Wright Sr., February 27, 1907, Boas Papers.

27. Boas, "Real Race Problem"; Franz Boas, "Race Problems in America," *Science*, 23.

28. Robert H. Lowie, review of *The Mind of Primitive Man*, by Franz Boas, *American Journal of Sociology* 17 (May 1912): 830–31.

29. Boas, foreword to Ovington, *Half a Man*, vii–viii.

30. Boas, "Human Faculty as Determined by Race," 240.

31. Frank H. Hankins, *The Racial Basis of Civilization* (New York: Knopf, 1926), 323–24.

32. Daniel G. Brinton, "The Aims of Anthropology," *Proceedings of the American Association for the Advancement of Science* 44 (December 1895): 12.

33. Hyatt, *Franz Boas—Social Activist*, 79.

34. Williams, *From a Caste to a Minority*, 69–73, 84–98.

35. Robert E. Park, "Education and Its Relation to the Conflict and Fusion of Cultures: With Special Reference to the Problems of the Immigrant, the Negro and Missions," *Publications of the American Sociological Society* 13 (December 1918): 40–41.

36. Frederick L. Hoffman, *Race Traits and Tendencies of the American Negro* (Philadelphia: American Economic Association, 1896), preface, 312, 188.

37. Kelly Miller, review of *Race Traits and Tendencies of the American Negro* by Frederick L. Hoffman, American Negro Academy occasional paper no. 1 (Washington, D.C.: American Negro Academy, 1897), 36.

38. W. E. B. Du Bois, review of *Race Traits and Tendencies of the American Negro* by Frederick L. Hoffman, *Annals* 9 (January 1897): 127–33.

39. W. E. B. Du Bois, *The Philadelphia Negro: A Social Study* (1899; reprint, New York: Schocken Books, 1967), 5–9.

40. W. E. B. Du Bois, "The Study of the Negro Problem," *Annals* 11 (January 1898): 19.

41. W. E. B. Du Bois to Franz Boas, October 11, 1905, and Franz Boas to W. E. B. Du Bois, October 14, 1905, Boas Papers.

42. W. E. B. Du Bois, ed., *The Health and Physique of the Negro American: Report of a Social Study Made under the Direction of Atlanta University; Together with the Proceedings of the Eleventh Conference for the Study of the Negro Problems, Held at Atlanta University on May the 29th, 1906,* Atlanta University publication no. 11 (Atlanta: Atlanta University Press, 1906), 27.

43. Quoted in Elliott M. Rudwick, *W. E. B. Du Bois: A Study in Minority Leadership* (Philadelphia: University of Pennsylvania Press, 1961), 123.

44. T. E. Taylor to Booker T. Washington, September 4, 1915, and Booker T. Washington to T. E. Taylor, September 14, 1915, Booker T. Washington Papers, Library of Congress, Washington, D.C.

45. Alain LeRoy Locke, "The Theoretical Scientific Conceptions of Race," in *Race Contacts and Interracial Relations,* ed. Jeffrey C. Stewart (Washington, D.C.: Howard University Press, 1992), 5–12.

46. George W. Ellis, "Psychology of American Race Prejudice," *Journal of Race Development* 6 (January 1915): 312; see also George W. Ellis, "The Negro in Democracy," *Journal of Race Development* 7 (July 1916): 78; and George W. Ellis, "Factors in the New American Race Situation," *Journal of Race Development* 8 (April 1917): 486. Ellis was aware of Boas's innovative thinking as early as 1907. See George W. Ellis to Franz Boas, May 28, 1907, Boas Papers.

47. Boas, "Human Faculty as Determined by Race," 226.

48. Franz Boas, "Industries of the African Negroes," *Southern Workman* 38 (April 1909): 225.

49. Franz Boas, *The Mind of Primitive Man* (New York: Macmillan, 1911), 272.

50. Franz Boas, "The Problem of the American Negro," *Yale Quarterly Review* 10 (January 1921): 386–87, 388–89, 390.

51. Franz Boas, "What Is Race?" *Nation,* January 28, 1925, 90–91.

52. Franz Boas, *Anthropology and Modern Life* (New York: Norton, 1928), 18, 38, 40.

53. Fredrickson, *The Arrogance of Race,* 179.

54. V. P. Franklin, "Black Social Scientists and the Mental Testing Movement, 1920–1940," in *Black Psychology,* 2nd ed., ed. Reginald L. Jones (New York: Harper and Row, 1980): 201–15.

55. Charles S. Johnson to Franz Boas, April 13, 1925, and Franz Boas to Charles S. Johnson, April 25, 1925, Boas Papers.

56. Abram Harris to Franz Boas, June 22, 1928, Charles H. Thompson to Franz Boas, June 23, 1928, and Franz Boas to Charles H. Thompson, July 5, 1928, Boas Papers.

57. Howard Hale Long to Franz Boas, March 13, 1929, and Franz Boas to Howard Hale Long, March 18, 1929, Boas Papers.

58. Lee D. Baker, *From Savage to Negro: Anthropology and the Construction of Race, 1896–1954* (Berkeley: University of California Press, 1998), 166–67.

59. George Hutchinson, *The Harlem Renaissance in Black and White* (Cambridge: Harvard University Press, 1995), 62–77.

60. Vernon J. Williams Jr., *Rethinking Race: Franz Boas and His Contemporaries* (Lexington: University Press of Kentucky, 1996); Genevieve Fabre and Michel Feith, *Temples for Tomorrow: Looking Back at the Harlem Renaissance* (Bloomington: Indiana University Press, 2001), 173–74.

61. Zora Neale Hurston, *Dust Tracks on a Road: An Autobiography* (New York: Lippincott, 1942), 123–25; Alain LeRoy Locke, ed., *The New Negro* (New York: Boni, 1925), 353–60; Margret M. Caffrey, *Ruth Benedict: Stranger in the Land* (Austin: University of Texas Press, 1989); Margaret Mead, *Blackberry Winter: My Earlier Years* (New York: Morrow, 1972). See also Dolores Janiewski and Lois W. Banner, eds., *Reading Benedict, Reading Mead: Feminism, Race, and Imperial Visions* (Baltimore: Johns Hopkins University Press, 2004).

62. Nathan I. Huggins, *Harlem Renaissance* (New York: Oxford University Press, 1971), 28.

63. Baker, *From Savage to Negro*, 166–67.

Chapter 3: A Gifted Amateur

Chapter 3 originally published as "A Gifted Amateur: The Case of George Washington Ellis," *American Anthropologist* 104 (June 2002): 554–60. © 2002 by the American Anthropological Association.

1. St. Clair Drake, "Anthropology and the Black Experience," *Black Scholar* 11, no. 7 (1980): 2–31.

2. Wilson J. Moses, *Afrotopia: The Roots of African American Popular History* (Cambridge, England: Cambridge University Press, 1998), 6.

3. Drake, "Anthropology and the Black Experience," 12–14.

4.. George W. Stocking Jr., *The Ethnographer's Magic and Other Essays in the History of Anthropology* (Madison: University of Wisconsin Press, 1992), 8.

5. I have used the label "amateur anthropologist" to describe George Washington Ellis, primarily because he was not employed by the government, museums, or universities to engage himself in ethnological research. Although Ellis communicated with distinguished persons in the aforementioned institutions, his ethnological research was a hobby or obsession.

6. It should be noted that from 1974 until 1990, St. Clair Drake examined and analyzed anthropology's history and the largely unknown role that persons of African ancestry played in the field. The history of African American ethnography has been explored most recently in works by historians Mia Bay and Wilson Jeremiah Moses and the historically minded anthropologists Carolyn Fluehr-Lobban, Ira E. Harrison and Faye Harrison, and Lee D. Baker.

7. George Washington Ellis, "Psychology in American Race Prejudice," *Journal of Race Development* 6 (January 1915): 312; Wilson J. Moses, *The Golden Age of Black Nationalism, 1850–1925* (Hamden, Conn.: Archon Books, 1978), 20–21, 59–61; George M. Fredrickson, *Black Liberation: A Comparative History of Black Ideologies in the United States and South Africa* (New York: Oxford University Press, 1995), 60; S. P. Fullinwider, *The Mind and Mood of Black America: Twentieth-Century Thought* (Homewood, Ill.: Dorsey Press,

1969); James T. Campbell, *Songs of Zion: The African American Episcopal Church in the United States and South Africa* (Chapel Hill: University of North Carolina Press, 1998); and Mia Bay, *The White Image in the Black Mind: African American Ideas about White People, 1830–1925* (New York: Oxford University Press, 2000). Evidence of varying, paradoxical strains of ethnology that were mixed with romanticism and the assertion of the redemptive power of Christianity to help "savages" progress toward civilization is found among the writings of members of the black elite. See Kevin K. Gaines, *Uplifting the Race: Black Leadership, Politics and Culture in the Twentieth Century* (Chapel Hill: University of North Carolina Press, 1996); and Lee D. Baker, "Research, Reform, and Racial Uplift: The Mission of the Hampton Folklore-Society, 1893–1899," *History of Anthropology* 9, no. 42 (2001): 42–80.

8. Rayford Logan and Michael Winston, "George Washington Ellis," in *The Dictionary of American Negro Biography* (New York: Norton, 1982), 211–12.

9. "Some Facts of George W. Ellis," Washington, D.C., and "Kansas Newspapers," n.d., Ellis Papers, Chicago Historical Society, Chicago (hereafter Ellis Papers).

10. Ibid.

11. Ibid.

12. Ellis was a diplomat in Liberia at a time when its economic resources were unknown. Furthermore, United States officials generally left the country to British mentorship. See Peter Duignan and L. H. Gann, *The United States and Africa* (Cambridge, England: Cambridge University Press, 1984). Ellis, however, made numerous attempts to encourage Americans to invest in the fledgling West African nation and to settle the boundary disputes between Britain and France. See Ellis to Arthur Barclay, August 8, 1904, Ellis to Theodore, July 27, 1905, and Ellis to Charles F. Scott, April 8, 1909, Ellis Papers.

13. George W. Ellis, "Education in Liberia," *Report of the Commissioner of Education* (Washington, D.C.: Government Printing Office, 1905), 111–29.

14. George W. Ellis to Otis T. Mason, April 4, 1906, Ellis Papers.

15. George W. Ellis to Franz Boas, May 28, 1907, Ellis Papers.

16. Ibid.

17. Franz Boas to George W. Ellis, August 28, 1907, Boas Papers.

18. George W. Ellis to W. E. B. Du Bois, July 15, 1908, Ellis Papers.

19. Walter Neale to George W. Ellis, January 18, 30, 1913, April 15, 25, 1914, Ellis Papers.

20. Regna Darnell, *And Along Came Boas: Continuity and Revolution in Americanist Anthropology* (Amsterdam: John Benjamin, 2000), 110.

21. George W. Ellis, *Negro Culture in West Africa: A Study of the Negro Group of Vai-Speaking People with Its Own Invented Alphabet and Written Language* (New York: Neale, 1914). Edward W. Blyden (1832–1912) was a promoter of the Back-to-Africa movement, a staunch supporter of the development of Liberia and Sierre Leone, and a gifted student of African languages, peoples, and customs. Blyden's most representative extant work is *African Life and Customs* (1908). Although he embraced a cultural absolutism for most of his adult life, by 1908 Blyden advocated what Wilson J. Moses calls a "relativistic multiculturalism." See Moses, *Afrotopia*, 131–35; see also Hollis Lynch, *Black Spokesman: Selected Published Writings of Edward Wilmot Blyden* (New York: Humanities Press, 1971). Alexander Crummell (1819–1898), the first person of African American descent to grad-

uate from Cambridge University, an ardent Pan-African nationalist, an Episcopalian missionary to Liberia, and the founder of the American Negro Academy, has in recent years emerged as a gargantuan figure in the history of African American thought and ideology. Crummell was a monoculturalist who rejected cultural relativism. See Moses, *Afrotopia*, and Wilson J. Moses, *Alexander Crummell: A Study of Civilization and Discontent* (New York: Oxford University Press, 1989); J. R. Oldfield, *Alexander Crummell (1819–1898) and the Creation of an African American Church in Liberia* (Lewiston, N.Y.: Mellen Press, 1990); Gregory U. Rigsby, *Alexander Crummell: Pioneer in Nineteenth-Century Pan-African Thought* (Westport, Conn.: Greenwood Press, 1987).

22. Ellis, *Negro Culture in West Africa*, 25, 273. Ellis's use of Boas's emphasis on the "native point of view" did not give attention to interracial differences of national status, class, gender, and ethnocultural differences.

23. Ibid., 273.

24. Ibid., 273–74.

25. Ibid.

26. Ralph E. Luker, *The Social Gospel in Black and White: American Racial Reform, 1885–1912* (Chapel Hill: University of North Carolina Press, 1991), 34–56.

27. Ellis, *Negro Culture in West Africa*, 128, 130, 135.

28. Moses, *Alexander Crummell*, 132.

29. Ellis, *Negro Culture in West Africa*, 85–109.

30. Ibid., 109.

31. Ibid.

32. Ellis, "An Address on the Protestant Episcopal Church as a Form in Liberian Education," December 8, 1909, Ellis Papers.

33. Ellis, *Negro Culture in West Africa*, 114.

34. Ibid., 268–69.

35. Ibid., 269–70.

36. Ibid., 119–20.

37. Ibid., 124.

38. W. E. B. Du Bois, review of *Negro Culture of West Africa* by George W. Ellis, *Crisis* 5 (February 1915): 199–200.

39. Robert Ezra Park, review of *Negro Culture of West Africa* by George W. Ellis, *American Journal of Sociology* 20 (May 1915): 841–42.

40. Walter Dyson, review of *Negro Culture of West Africa* by George W. Ellis, *Journal of Negro History* 1 (1916): 95.

41. John Hope Franklin, *From Slavery to Freedom* (New York: McGraw-Hill, 1994), 519; Drake, "Anthropology and the Black Experience," 2.

42. Duignan and Gann, *United States and Africa*, 411.

Chapter 4: The Internalist-Externalist Controversy in the History of Racial Thought

Chapter 4 reprinted from the appendix in *From a Caste to a Minority: Changing Attitudes of American Sociologists toward Afro-Americans, 1896–1945*, by Vernon Williams Jr.

1. E. Franklin Frazier, "Sociological Theory and Race Relations," *American Sociological Review* 12 (June 1947): 269.

2. Vernon J. Williams Jr., *Rethinking Race: Franz Boas and His Contemporaries* (Lexington: University Press of Kentucky, 1996); Vernon J. Williams Jr., *From a Caste to a Minority: Changing Attitudes of American Sociologists toward Afro-Americans, 1896–1945* (Westport, Conn.: Greenwood Press, 1989).

3. Thomas F. Gossett, *Race: The History of an Idea in America* (Dallas: Southern Methodist University Press, 1963), 423–30.

4. George W. Stocking Jr., *Race, Culture, and Evolution: Essays in the History of Anthropology* (New York: Free Press, 1968), 303, 307; Nancy Stepan, *The Idea of Race in Science: Great Britain, 1800–1860* (London: Macmillan, 1982). Stepan concurred with Stocking's internalist perspective, arguing that "social and political factors . . . did not determine directly the specific form scientific arguments took about race. These arguments were instead derived from the procedures and content of the sciences themselves" (xv–xvi). Unwittingly, Professor Stepan's book suggests that British scientists and social scientists were unable or unwilling to pursue a more enlightened path on the issue of race at the beginning of the twentieth century because there were not sufficient demographic and social structural changes in their nation.

5. Leonard Lieberman, "The Debate over Race: A Study in the Sociology of Knowledge," in *Race and IQ*, ed. Ashley Montagu (New York: Oxford University Press, 1975), 30.

6. Marvin Harris, *The Rise of Anthropological Theory* (New York: Crowell, 1968), 297. For a fuller statement of Harris's position, see his *Theories of Culture in Postmodern Times* (Lanham, Md.: Alta Mira Press, 1999), 67–73.

7. Hamilton Cravens, *The Triumph of Evolution: American Scientists and the Heredity-Environment Controversy, 1900–1941* (Philadelphia: University of Pennsylvania Press, 1978), 92.

8. Williams, *Rethinking Race*, 92.

Chapter 5: Booker T. Washington

Chapter 5 reprinted from *A Different Vision: African American Economic Thought*, ed. Thomas D. Boston, by permission of Thomas D. Boston.

1. Booker T. Washington, *Up from Slavery* (1901; reprint, New York: Penguin Books, 1986), 219.

2. Ibid., 221.

3. Ibid., 220.

4. Ibid.

5. Ibid., 218.

6. Ibid., 218–19.

7. Ibid., 220.

8. Ibid., 221–22.

9. Ibid., 223.

10. August Meier, *Negro Thought in America, 1880–1915: Racial Ideologies in the Age of Booker T. Washington* (1963; reprint, Ann Arbor: University of Michigan Press, 1964), 110–14; Louis R. Harlan, *Booker T. Washington: The Making of a Black Leader, 1856–1901* (New York: Oxford University Press, 1972), 298–99.

11. Robert E. Park, lectures from a course entitled "The Negro in America" at the University of Chicago, 1931. Robert E. Park Papers, Regenstein Library, Chicago, 31–32.

12. Ibid., 31.

13. Ibid., 32.

14. Ibid., 31.

15. Ibid., 31.

16. Ibid., 32.

17. Ibid., 31.

18. Washington, *Up from Slavery,* 16.

19. Booker T. Washington, *Frederick Douglass* (1907; reprint, New York: Haskell House, 1968), 5.

20. George M. Fredrickson, *The Black Image in the White Mind: The Debate on Afro-American Character and Destiny, 1817–1914* (New York: Harper and Row, 1971).

21. Booker T. Washington, *The Negro in the South: His Economic Progress in Relation to His Moral and Religious Development* (1909; reprint, New York: Carol, 1970), 74–75.

22. Ibid., 40.

23. Booker T. Washington, *The Future of the American Negro* (1899; reprint, New York: Haskell House, 1968), 6–7.

24. Washington, *Up from Slavery,* 80.

25. Ibid., 83.

26. Washington, *The Future of the American Negro,* 13–14.

27. Washington, *Up from Slavery,* 85–86.

28. Meier, *Negro Thought in America,* 85.

29. Wilson J. Moses, *The Golden Age of Black Nationalism, 1850–1925* (1978; reprint, New York: Oxford University Press, 1988), 93.

30. Ibid.

31. E. Washington, ed., *Selected Speeches of Booker T. Washington* (Garden City, N.Y.: Doubleday, Doran, 1932), 277.

32. Ibid., 277.

33. Meier, *Negro Thought in America,* 86.

34. Emma Lou Thornborough, ed., *Booker T. Washington* (Englewood Cliffs, N.J.: Prentice-Hall, 1990), 157.

35. Franz Boas to Booker T. Washington, November 30, 1904, Boas Papers.

36. Ibid.

37. Ibid.

38. Booker T. Washington to Franz Boas, December 9, 1904, Boas Papers.

39. Robert E. Hemenway, *Zora Neale Hurston: A Literary Biography* (Urbana: University of Illinois Press, 1972), 206, 214.

40. Franz Boas to Booker T. Washington, November 8, 1906, and Booker T. Washington to Franz Boas, June 17, 1912, Boas Papers.

41. Linda O. McMurray, *Recorder of the Black Experience: A Biography of Monroe Nathan Work* (Baton Rouge: Louisiana State University Press, 1985), 60.

42. "Monroe Nathan Work," Jessie P. Guzman Papers, Tuskegee University, Tuskegee, Alabama.

43. Monroe N. Work, "An Autobiographical Sketch," February 7, 1940, Monroe N. Work Papers, Tuskegee University, Tuskegee, Alabama (hereafter Work Papers).

44. Booker T. Washington, *The Story of the Negro: The Rise of the Race from Slavery*, 2 vols. (1909; reprint, New York: Peter Smith, 1940), 1:32, 47, 50, 58, 59, 71, 74, 75.

45. Robert E. Park to Booker T. Washington, June 2, 1905, Booker T. Washington Papers, Library of Congress, Washington, D.C. (hereafter Washington Papers).

46. Robert E. Park, *Race and Culture* (New York: Free Press, 1950), vii–viii.

47. John H. Stanfield, *Philanthropy and Jim Crow in American Social Science* (Westport, Conn.: Greenwood Press, 1985), 42.

48. Robert E. Park to Booker T. Washington, June 2, 1908, Washington Papers.

49. Washington, *The Story of the Negro*, 1:5–6.

50. Ibid., 1:8–9.

51. Ibid., 1:24.

52. Quoted in Charles Breasted, *Pioneer of the Past: The Story of James Henry Breasted, Archaeologist* (New York: Scribner's, 1943), 176.

53. Booker T. Washington to James H. Breasted, May 6, 1909, Washington Papers.

Chapter 6: Ulysses G. Weatherly

1. Donald N. Levine, *Visions of the Sociological Tradition* (Chicago: University of Chicago Press, 1995), 8–9.

2. James B. McKee, *Sociology and the Race Problem: The Failure of a Perspective* (Urbana: University of Illinois Press, 1993), 349–50.

3. Vernon J. Williams Jr., *From a Caste to a Minority: Changing Attitudes of American Sociologists toward Afro-Americans, 1896–1945* (Westport, Conn.: Greenwood Press, 1989), 180.

4. E. Franklin Frazier, "Sociological Theory and Race Relations," *American Sociological Review* 12 (June 1947): 269.

5. George M. Fredrickson, *The Black Image in the White Mind: Historical Perspectives on Slavery, Racism, and Social Inequality* (Middletown, Conn.: Wesleyan University Press, 1988).

6. McKee, *Sociology and the Race Problem*, 55–102.

7. Emma Lou Thornbrough, *The Negro in Indiana: A Study of a Minority* (Indianapolis: Indiana Historical Bureau, 1985), 229.

8. Weatherly, discussion of "Race Friction," by Alfred Holt Stone, *American Journal of Sociology* 13 (May 1908): 824.

9. Weatherly did not retain his personal and professional correspondence. As a consequence, the biographical vignette I have composed is based on material gathered in the Ulysses G. Weatherly Papers, Indiana University Archives, Bloomington (hereafter Weatherly Papers). Delores M. Lahrman to Chancellor Herman B. Wells, October 9, 1985, Weatherly Papers. Howard W. Odum, *American Sociology: The Story of Sociology in the United States through 1950* (New York: Longmans, Green, 1951), 126–28.

10. Anonymous, *Centennial Tour of Historical Places Associated with Indiana University Sociology*, 1885–1985, 1 [brochure, located at Indiana University Archives, Bloomington].

11. Anonymous, "Professor U. G. Weatherly Speaks Concerning Race Problem," *Daily Student*, January, 26, 1905.

12. Weatherly, discussion of "Race Friction," 324.

13. Ibid.

14. Ulysses G. Weatherly, "A World-Wide Color Line," *Popular Science* 79 (November 1911): 481.

15. Ulysses G. Weatherly, "The First Universal Races Congress," *American Journal of Sociology* 17 (November 1911): 324–25.

16. Ibid.

17. Ulysses G. Weatherly, "Racial Pessimism," *Publications of the American Sociological Society* 18 (December 1923): 12.

18. Ulysses G. Weatherly, "Race and Marriage," *American Journal of Sociology* 15 (January 1910): 445–47.

19. Howard W. Odum, *Social and Mental Traits of the Negro* (New York: University, 1910), 287–88.

20. Weatherly, "Race and Marriage," 444.

21. Ibid., 444.

22. Ibid., 444.

23. Ibid., 448–49.

24. Ibid., 448.

25. Gunnar Myrdal, *An American Dilemma,* 2 vols. (New York: Harper and Row, 1944), 2: 60.

26. Ulysses G. Weatherly, *Social Progress* (Philadelphia: Lippincott, 1926), 127.

27. Ibid., 135–36.

28. Ulysses G. Weatherly to William Lowe Bryan, March 27, April 26, 29, 1926, Weatherly Papers.

29. Ulysses G. Weatherly, "The West Indies as a Sociological Laboratory," *American Journal of Sociology* 29 (November 1923): 296.

30. Ibid., 303.

Chapter 7: A Kind of Conservative

Chapter 7 originally published as "Monroe N. Work's Contribution to Booker T. Washington's Nationalist Legacy," *Western Journal of Black Studies* 21 (summer 1997): 85–91. © 1997 by the Washington State University Press.

1. Ralph E. Luker, *The Social Gospel in Black and White: American Racial Reform* (Chapel Hill: University of North Carolina Press, 1991), 268, 323.

2. George M. Fredrickson, *Black Liberation: A Comparative History of Black Ideologies in the United States and South Africa* (New York: Oxford University Press, 1995), 35.

3. August Meier, *Negro Thought in America, 1880–1915: Racial Ideologies in the Age of Booker T. Washington* (1963; reprint, Ann Arbor: University of Michigan Press, 1964), 16, 23–24; Jessie P. Guzman, "Monroe Nathan Work and His Contributions," *Journal of Negro History* 34 (October 1949): 431; Linda O. McMurry, *Recorder of the Black Experience: A Biography of Monroe Nathan Work* (Baton Rouge: Louisiana State University Press, 1985), 12–15; Kevin K. Gaines, *Uplifting the Race: Black Leadership, Politics, and Culture in the Twentieth Century* (Chapel Hill: University of North Carolina Press, 1996), 32–33. In his pioneering and magisterial historical investigation of the thought of the African American leadership class, August Meier argued in 1963 that during the years between the end of the Civil War and the turn of the twentieth century, African Americans ex-

changed one version of the regnant success myths for another. During Reconstruction, Meier stated, "the masses were primarily interested in land ownership," while the "elite leaders, who had achieved some sort of economic security, were first and foremost interested in political and civil rights." By the end of the century, Meier noted, African Americans had jettisoned the latter approach and adopted the "ideas of the gospel of wealth and Social Darwinism," which they applied to their own racial situation. Nevertheless, Meier admits that African Americans "never abandoned their emphasis upon the Christian and humanitarian and democratic elements in the American tradition."

Meier also could have argued that the vision of education was as significant in the former slaves' minds as land ownership, for education was seen as an indispensable means to socioeconomic advancement. The vision of education also underwent a transition at the same time that the dream of land ownership augmented. As the historian Kevin K. Gaines has pointed out correctly, the emancipatory vision of education changed from the classical liberal training to industrial education, which emphasized moral and economic progress.

4. James R. Grossman, *Land of Hope: Chicago, Black Southerners, and the Great Migration* (Chicago: University of Chicago Press, 1989), 32–33.

5. Barbara Ballis Lal, "The 'Chicago School' of American Sociology, Symbolic Interactionism, and Race Relations Theory," in *Theories of Race and Ethnic Relations,* ed. John Rex and David Mason (Cambridge, England: Cambridge University Press, 1986), 282; Grossman, *Land of Hope,* 32.

6. Grossman, *Land of Hope,* 33.

7. McMurry, *Recorder of the Black Experience,* 12–15; Guzman, "Monroe Nathan Work and His Contributions," 431.

8. Robert Higgs, *Competition and Coercion* (Cambridge, England: Cambridge University Press, 1977), 10; John Mark Tucker, "'You Can't Argue with Facts': Monroe Nathan Work as Information Officer, Editor, and Bibliographer," paper in the possession of this author, 3.

9. Quoted in McMurry, *Recorder of the Black Experience,* 15.

10. McMurry, *Recorder of the Black Experience,* 15.

11. McMurry, *Recorder of the Black Experience,* 12–15.

12. Guzman, "Monroe Nathan Work and His Contributions," 431. The best and most in-depth study of the Exodusters is still Nell and Irwin Painter, *Exodusters: Black Migration to Kansas after Reconstruction* (New York: Knopf, 1966).

13. James T. Campbell, *Songs of Zion: The African Methodist Episcopal Church in the United States and South Africa* (Chapel Hill: University of North Carolina Press, 1998), 38–43.

14. George M. Fredrickson, *Black Liberation: A Comparative History of Black Ideologies in the United States and South Africa* (New York: Oxford University Press, 1995), 78.

15. Wilson Jeremiah Moses, *The Golden Age of Black Nationalism, 1850–1925* (Hamden, Conn.: Shoe String Press, 1978), 11, 30.

16. Campbell, *Songs of Zion,* 43.

17. Guzman, "Monroe Nathan Work and His Contributions," 432; McMurry, *Recorder of the Black Experience,* 16–17.

18. Guzman, "Monroe Nathan Work and His Contributions," 432; McMurry, *Recorder of the Black Experience,* 17.

19. Fredrickson, *Black Liberation,* 76. For an explanation of the concept of "social control," which was first formulated by one of the "fathers" of sociology, Edward Alworth Ross, see Edgar F. Borgatta and Henry J. Meyer, eds., *Social Control and the Foundations of Sociology: Pioneer Contributions of Edward Alworth Ross to the Study of Society* (Boston: Beacon Press, 1959).

20. Meier, *Negro Thought in America,* 16, 23–24; Gaines, *Uplifting the Race,* 32–33.

21. Louise C. Wade, *Graham Taylor: Pioneer for Social Justice, 1851–1938* (Chicago: University of Chicago Press, 1964), 1–82; Luker, *The Social Gospel in Black and White,* 173–74.

22. Charles H. Hopkins, *The Rise of the Social Gospel in American Protestantism, 1865–1915* (New Haven: Yale University Press, 1940), 321.

23. Quoted in Guzman, "Monroe Nathan Work and His Contributions," 432.

24. McMurry, *Recorder of the Black Experience,* 18–19.

25. Donald N. Levine, *Visions of the Sociological Tradition* (Chicago: University of Chicago Press, 1995), 251.

26. Nathan Work, "Sociology in the Common School," *Proceedings of the American Sociological Society* 13 (December 1918): 96–97.

27. W. E. B. Du Bois, *The Philadelphia Negro: A Social Study* (1899; reprint, New York: Schocken Books, 1967), 5–9.

28. Vernon J. Williams Jr., "A Gifted Amateur: The Case of George Washington Ellis," *American Anthropologist* (June 2002): 544.

29. Luker, *The Social Gospel in Black and White,* 173–74.

30. Ibid.

31. Reverdy C. Ransom, *The Pilgrimage of Harriet Ransom's Son* (Nashville: A.M.E. Sunday School Union, c. 1948); Reverdy C. Ransom, *The Spirit of Freedom and Justice* (Nashville: A.M.E. Sunday School Union, 1926).

32. Ransom, *The Pilgrimage of Harriet Ransom's Son,* 106.

33. Richard R. Wright Jr., *Eighty-Seven Years behind the Black Curtain: An Autobiography* (Philadelphia: Rare Books, 1965), 1–40.

34. Monroe N. Work, "Monroe N. Work," Work Papers.

35. Wright, *Eighty-Seven Years behind the Black Curtain,* 49.

36. For biographical information on William I. Thomas, see Paul J. Baker, ed., "The Life Histories of W. I. Thomas and Robert E. Park," *American Journal of Sociology* 79 (September 1973): 247–48. Morris Janowitz, introduction to *W. I. Thomas on Social Organization and Social Personality: Selected Papers,* ed. Morris Janowitz (Chicago: University of Chicago Press, 1966), vi–vii.

37. Vernon J. Williams Jr., *From a Caste to a Minority: Changing Attitudes of American Sociologists toward Afro-Americans, 1896–1945* (Westport, Conn.: Greenwood Press, 1989), 45–46, 72–73.

38. Work, unpublished article, 1908, Work Papers.

39. William I. Thomas, *Source Book for Social Origins: Ethnological Materials, Psychological Standpoint, Classified and Annotated Bibliographies for the Interpretation of Savage Society* (Chicago: University of Chicago Press, 1909), ii–12.

40. Tucker, "'You Can't Argue with Facts.'"

41. Work, "Monroe Nathan Work."

42. Frederick L. Hoffman, *Race Traits and Tendencies of the American Negro* (Philadelphia: American Economic Association, 1896), preface.

43. George M. Fredrickson, *The Black Image in the White Mind: Historical Perspectives on Slavery, Racism, and Social Inequality* (Middletown, Conn.: Wesleyan University Press, 1988), 255; Joel Williamson, *A Rage for Order: Black-White Relations in the American South since Emancipation* (New York: Oxford University Press, 1986), 71–72.

44. Kelly Miller, review of *Race Traits and Tendencies of the American Negro* by Frederick L. Hoffman, American Negro Academy occasional paper no. 1 (Washington, D.C.: American Negro Academy, 1897).

45. W. E. B. Du Bois, review of *Race Traits and Tendencies* by Frederick L. Hoffman, *Annals of the American Academy of Political and Social Sciences* 9 (January 1897): 127–33.

46. Ibid.

47. Monroe N. Work, "Crime among the Negroes of Chicago," *American Journal of Sociology* 6 (September 1900): 222–23.

48. Ibid.

49. Monroe N. Work, "The Negro Real Estate Owners of Chicago" (M.A. thesis, University of Chicago, 1903), 1–4.

50. Ibid., 4.

51. Ibid., 6–28.

52. Ibid., 28.

53. Ibid., 31.

54. Monroe N. Work, "An Autobiographical Sketch (Monroe Nathan Work)," typescript, February 7, 1940, Work Papers.

55. W. E. B. Du Bois and Monroe N. Work, "The Middle West, Illinois," in *The Negro Church*, ed. W. E. B. Du Bois (Atlanta: Atlanta University Press, 1903), 83–93.

56. Monroe N. Work, "The Negro Brain," in *The Health and Physique of the Negro American: Report of a Social Study Made under the Direction of Atlanta University; Together with the Proceedings of the Eleventh Conference for the Study of the Negro Problems, Held at Atlanta University on May the 29th, 1906*, ed. W. E. B. Du Bois, Atlanta University publication no. 11 (Atlanta: Atlanta University Press, 1906), 25–27.

57. The *Southern Workman* was a periodical founded in January 1872 by General Samuel Chapman Armstrong, Booker T. Washington's major mentor and source of inspiration. It was initially designed to address the practical affairs of the freed people. It eventually became a propaganda organ for Hampton graduates and an invaluable source of history, culture, and national and world news that affected African Americans. See Virginia Lantz Denton, *Booker T. Washington and the Adult Education Movement* (Gainesville: University Press of Florida, 1993), 71–72.

58. Monroe Nathan Work, "Monroe Nathan Work, Director of Department of Research and Records, Tuskegee Institute, 1908," typescript, 1908, Work Papers.

59. Monroe N. Work, "An Autobiographical Sketch (Monroe Nathan Work)."

60. Monroe N. Work, "Booker T. Washington, Pioneer," *Journal of Social Forces* 3 (January 1925): 310.

61. Booker T. Washington to Monroe Nathan Work, November 9, 15, 1910, Monroe Nathan Work to Booker T. Washington, December 20, 1910, Booker T. Washington to Monroe Nathan Work, August 8, 1911, Monroe Nathan Work to Booker T. Washington,

January 3, 1911, Booker T. Washington to Emmett Jay Scott, November 23, 1911, Booker T. Washington to Monroe Nathan Work, May 20, 1912, and Monroe Nathan Work to Booker T. Washington, July 16, 17, 1914, February 6, 1915, Washington Papers.

62. Booker T. Washington to Monroe Nathan Work, November 15, 1910, Washington Papers.

63. Ibid.

64. Louis R. Harlan, introduction to *The Booker T. Washington Papers,* vol. 1, ed. Louis R. Harlan (Urbana: University of Illinois Press, 1972), xxxvii.

65. Quoted in McMurry, *Recorder of the Black Experience,* 60.

66. Monroe N. Work, "The Passing Tradition and African Civilization," *Journal of Negro History* 1 (January 1916): 32.

67. Ibid., 32.

68. Ibid., 41.

69. Ibid.

70. Ibid.

71. For biographical information on Alexander Crummell, see Gregory U. Rigsby, *Alexander Crummell: Pioneer in Nineteenth-Century Pan-African Thought* (Westport, Conn.: Greenwood Press, 1988); Wilson J. Moses, *Alexander Crummell: A Study of Civilization and Discontent* (New York: Oxford University Press, 1989); and J. R. Oldfield, ed., *Alexander Crummell on the South* (Charlottesville: University Press of Virginia, 1995).

72. Work, "The Passing Tradition and African Civilization," 42.

73. Monroe N. Work, "A Half Century of Progress: The Negro in America in 1866 and 1922," *Missionary of the World Review* 45 (June 1922): 431–40; "Aspects and Tendencies of the Race Problem (1912–24)," *Publications of the American Sociological Society* 19 (December 29–31, 1924): 191–96; "The Economic Progress of the Negro," typescript, December 31, 1929, Work Papers; "Cooperation and the South's New Economic Conditions," typescript, [1928], Work Papers; "Two Generations since Emancipation," *Missionary Review of the World* 59 (June 1936).

74. Work, "Aspects and Tendencies of the Race Problem," 191–96.

75. Ibid.

76. Monroe N. Work, untitled, typescript, n.d., Work Papers.

77. Ibid.

78. Monroe N. Work, "Racial Factors and Economic Forces in Land Tenure in the South," *Journal of Social Forces* 15 (December 19, 1936): 215.

79. Monroe N. Work, "Problems of Adjustment of Race and Class in the South," *Journal of Social Forces* 16 (October 1937): 117.

80. E. Franklin Frazier to W. E. B. Du Bois, November 7, 1936, W. E. B. Du Bois Archives, University of Massachusetts at Amherst.

Conclusion

Conclusion originally published as "Racial Essentialism: A Case of Historical Continuity and Discontinuity in the Social Sciences," *Western Journal of Black Studies* 25 (winter 2001): 201–10. © 2001 by Washington State University Press.

1. Vernon J. Williams Jr., "W. E. B. Du Bois and E. Franklin Frazier: Exposing the Pitfalls of Prejudiced Social Science," *Griot* 15 (fall 1996): 14.

2. William G. McLoughlin, syllabus for History 178A: The Social and Intellectual History of the United States, 1789–1865, Brown University, fall 1991, 1 [given to author in 1992 by William G. McLoughlin]; Vernon J. Williams Jr., review of *A Right to Sing the Blues: African Americans, Jews, and American Popular Song* by Jeffrey Melnick, *Shofar* 20 (fall 2001): 175–77.

3. George M. Fredrickson, *The Arrogance of Race: Historical Perspectives on Slavery, Racism, and Social Inequality* (Middletown, Conn.: Wesleyan University Press, 1988), 179.

4. Wilson J. Moses, *Afrotopia: The Roots of African American Popular History* (Cambridge, England: Cambridge University Press, 1998), 241.

5. W. E. B. Du Bois, *The Negro* (1915; reprint, New York: Oxford University Press, 1970), 7.

6. Maghan Keita, *Race and the Writing of History: Riddling the Sphinx* (New York: Oxford University Press, 2000), 36. Professor Keita also has argued persuasively that the complicity of African American historians with European American scholars in contributing to the racial essentialist narratives of their respective races has resulted in the shunting of African American historians' intellectual lives "to a junction labeled 'Blacks Only'" (36).

7. Rayford W. Logan, *The Negro in American Life and Thought: The Nadir, 1877–1901* (London: Dial Press, 1954); enlarged edition published as *The Betrayal of the Negro: From Rutherford B. Hayes to Woodrow Wilson* (London: Collier Books, 1965).

8. See, for example, Linda O. McMurry, *George Washington Carver: Scientist and Symbol* (New York: Oxford University Press, 1981); Kenneth R. Manning, *Black Apollo of Science: The Life of Ernest Just* (New York: Oxford University Press, 1983); John Hope Franklin, *George Washington Williams: A Biography* (Chicago: University of Chicago Press, 1985); Linda O. McMurry, *Recorder of the Black Experience: A Biography of Monroe Nathan Work* (Baton Rouge: Louisiana State University Press, 1985); Vernon J. Williams Jr., review of *Recorder of the Black Experience: A Biography of Monroe Nathan Work* by Linda O. McMurry, *Afro-Americans in New York Life and History* 12 (July 1988): 59–60; Jacqueline Anne Rouse, *Lugenia Burns Hope: Black Southern Reformer* (Athens: University of Georgia Press, 1989); David Levering Lewis, *W. E. B. Du Bois: Biography of a Race, 1868–1919* (New York: Holt, 1993); Vernon J. Williams Jr., review of *W. E. B. Du Bois: Biography of Race, 1868–1919* by David Levering Lewis, *Explorations in Sights and Sounds* 14 (summer 1994): 48–49; Dickson D. Bruce Jr., *Archibald Grimké: Portrait of a Black Independent* (Baton Rouge: Louisiana State University Press, 1993); Vernon J. Williams Jr., review of *Archibald Grimké: Portrait of a Black Independent* by Dickson D. Bruce Jr., *Explorations in Sights and Sounds* 15 (summer 1995): 33–34; Jacqueline Goggin, *Carter G. Woodson: A Life in Black History* (Baton Rouge: Louisiana State University Press, 1993); Vernon J. Williams Jr., review of *Carter G. Woodson: A Life in Black History* by Jacqueline Goggin, *Afro-Americans in New York Life and History* 18 (July 1994): 59–60; Linda O. McMurry, *To Keep the Waters Troubled: The Life of Ida B. Wells* (New York: Oxford University Press, 1998); John David Smith, *Black Judas: William Hannibal Thomas and the American Negro* (Athens: University of Georgia Press, 2000); Vernon J. Williams Jr., review of *Black Judas: William Hannibal Thomas and the American Negro* by John David Smith, *Journal of American History* 88 (September 2001): 667–68.

9. Du Bois, *The Negro*, 7.

10. Audrey Smedley, *Race in North America: Origins and Evolutions of a Worldview* (Boulder, Colo.: Westview Press, 1993), 25–29.

11. Chris Smaje, *Natural Hierarchies: The Historical Sociology of Race and Caste* (Malden, Mass.: Blackwell, 2000), 4.

12. Ibid., 256–58.

13. James B. McKee, *Sociology and the Race Problem: A Failure in Perspective* (Urbana: University of Illinois Press, 1993), 342–43.

14. W. Lloyd Warner, "American Caste and Class," *American Journal of Sociology* 41 (September 1936): 234–37; "A Methodological Note," in St. Claire Drake and Horace R. Cayton, *Black Metropolis* (New York: Harcourt, Brace, 1945), 774, 782; W. Lloyd Warner and Allison Davis, *A Comparative Study of American Caste, in Race Relations and the Race Problem* (New York: Greenwood Press, 1968), 229–34; W. Lloyd Warner, Buford H. Junker, and Walter A. Adams, *Color and Human Nature* (Washington, D.C.: American Council on Education, 1941); Hortense Powdermaker, *After Freedom* (New York: Viking Press, 1939).

15. Smaje, *Natural Hierarchies,* 3.

16. Lee D. Baker, *From Savage to Negro: Anthropology and the Construction of Race, 1896–1945* (Berkeley: University of California Press, 1998).

17. Sander L. Gilman and Nancy Leys Stepan, "Appropriating the Idioms of Science: The Rejection of Scientific Racism," in *The Bounds of Race: Perspectives on Hegemony and Resistance,* ed. Dominick La Capra (Ithaca, N.Y.: Cornell University Press, 1991), 72–103; Moses, *Afrotopia,* 96–135, 226–41; Baker, *From Savage to Negro;* Ira Harrison and Faye Harrison, eds., *African-American Pioneers in Anthropology* (Urbana: University of Illinois Press, 1999); Carolyn Fluehr-Lobban, "Anténor Firmin: Haitian Pioneer of Anthropology," *American Anthropologist* 102 (September 2000): 449–64, and the introduction to *The Equality of the Human Races,* translated by Asselin Charles (New York: Garland, 2000); Mia Bay, *The White Image in the Black Mind: African-American Ideas about White People, 1830–1925* (New York: Oxford University Press, 2000), 38–74.

Index

VERNON J. WILLIAMS JR. is a professor of African American and African Diaspora studies and American studies at Indiana University in Bloomington, and is the author of *From a Caste to a Minority* (1989) and *Rethinking Race* (1996). Formerly the editor of the *New England Journal of Black Studies,* he is currently on the editorial boards of the *Western Journal of Black Studies* and the *Journal of African American Studies* and contributing editor to *Transforming Anthropology.*

Williams has received fellowships or grants from the American Association for the Advancement of Science Section on Anthropology, the Indiana Historical Society, Indiana University, Purdue University, the American Council of Learned Societies, the Afro-American Studies Center of Boston University, the National Endowment for the Humanities, the William Monroe Trotter Institute, and Rhode Island College.

The University of Illinois Press
is a founding member of the
Association of American University Presses.

Composed in 10.5/13 Adobe Minion
by Jim Proefrock
at the University of Illinois Press
Manufactured by Thomson-Shore, Inc.

University of Illinois Press
1325 South Oak Street
Champaign, IL 61820-6903
www.press.uillinois.edu